It's another great book from CGP...

If you're studying Design & Technology at KS3 (ages 11-14), this CGP book explains all the skills and processes you'll need to understand — and how to apply them.

There's also plenty of essential background information, covering everything from design and development to production and industry.

CGP — still the best! ☺

Our sole aim here at CGP is to produce the highest quality books — carefully written, immaculately presented and dangerously close to being funny.

Then we work our socks off to get them out to you — at the cheapest possible prices.

Contents

Section 1 — Research and Analysis

Design Briefs and Research 1
Inspiration For Design 2
Analysing Products and Technology 4
Research and the Internet 5
Understanding Needs 6
Targeted Research 7
New Products and Technologies 8
The Impact of Technology 9

Section 2 — Development and Evaluation

Design Specifications 10
Planning 11
Modelling 13
Presenting Ideas 15
Evaluating and Adapting Designs 16
Product Evolution and Design Movements 17

Section 3 — Production and Industry

Scale of Production 18
Batch Production 19
Quality and Accuracy 20
Manufacturing and Processing 21
Industry 22
Computer-Aided Manufacture 23
The Food Industry 24
Manufacturing and Industry 25
CNC Machines 26
Health and Safety 27
Environmental Concerns 28

Section 4 — Resistant Materials

Classifying Materials 30
Selecting Materials 31
Modern Materials 32
Changing Properties 33
Testing the Properties of Materials 34
Finishing Techniques & the Environment 35
Joining 36
Forming 37
Tools and Equipment 38

Section 5 — Textiles

Classifying Materials 40
World Materials 41
Selecting Materials 42
Testing Properties 43
Modern Materials 44
Processing Materials 45
Techniques 46
More Techniques 47
Tools and Equipment 48

Section 6 — Cooking and Nutrition

Nutrition 49
Healthy Eating 50
Selecting Ingredients 51
Properties of Ingredients 52
Modern Ingredients 53
Sourcing Ingredients 54
Additives 55
Processing Ingredients 56
Food Processing 57
Planning a Meal 58
Cooking Methods 59
Cooking Equipment 62

Section 7 — Control and Design & Technology

Systems and Control 64
Circuits and PCBs 65
Motion and Mechanisms 66
More Mechanical Systems 67
Strong Structures 68
Computer-Controlled Systems 69
Security Control 70
Monitoring and Display Systems 71

Glossary 72

Index 74

Published by CGP

Editors:
Gordon Henderson, Rachael Marshall, Matteo Orsini Jones, Sophie Scott and Sarah Williams.

Contributors:
John Cash and Jane Scott.

ISBN: 978 1 841467 207

With thanks to Jane Allen, Paul Anderson and Rachel Kordan for the proofreading.
With thanks to Laura Jakubowski for the copyright research.

Thanks to Science Photo Library for permission to use the images on pages 3, 4, 13, and 17.
Thanks to iStockphoto.com for permission to use the images on pages 3 and 22.
Image of The Eden Project on page 3 by A1personage, Wikimedia Commons.
Photograph on page 17 "Carlton" by Ettore Sottsass 1981 – Memphis Milano Collection. Pariano Angelantonio courtesy of Memphis Milano.
With thanks to TechSoft UK Ltd for permission to use photographs of CNC machines on page 26.

Every effort has been made to locate copyright holders and obtain permission to reproduce sources. For those sources where it has been difficult to trace the originator of the work, we would be grateful for information. If any copyright holder would like us to make an amendment to the acknowledgements, please notify us and we will gladly update the book at the next reprint. Thank you.

Clipart from Corel®
Printed by Elanders Ltd, Newcastle upon Tyne.

Based on the classic CGP style created by Richard Parsons.

Text, design, layout and original illustrations © Coordination Group Publications Ltd. (CGP) 2014
All rights reserved.

Photocopying more than one chapter of this book is not permitted. Extra copies are available from CGP with next day delivery.
0800 1712 712 • www.cgpbooks.co.uk

Section 1 — Research and Analysis

Design Briefs and Research

All great products must start with a design brief — otherwise, how would you know what you're supposed to be making? Read on and you'll learn all about how you could come up with ideas for products.

Designing Starts with the Design Brief

So, someone gets an idea for a new product.
They decide to employ a designer to work on the idea.

1) The person who hires the designer is called the client.
2) The client gives the designer a design brief...
3) The design brief is a starting point for the development of the product. It should include:

- What kind of product is needed (and why)
- How the product will be used, and where (what environment)
- Who the product is for (the target market)

DESIGN BRIEF FOR SCREWDRIVER / DOG WHISTLE
There are currently no dog whistles that have the capacity to double-up as a screwdriver. We want you to design a product to meet this need for people who want to keep their dog in check while fixing loose door hinges in dog salons.

You Can Come Up with the Design Brief Yourself

1) Design briefs don't always have to come from a client.
2) You might have come up with an idea or design brief yourself, because you saw a gap in the market or you really want something that isn't available.
3) It's still important to write down the usual things that a design brief includes. This stops you forgetting important points further down the line, and it makes it easier for anyone helping you out on the project to understand your aims.
4) You could also come up with a design based on a context, rather than a product. E.g. 'I want to check all of my email accounts without having to sign in and out of each one'. You can then design a product that's useful in this situation. This is known as context design.

A 'gap in the market' means a product could sell well, but nobody's actually selling it.

Research What People Want and Need

1) Once you've got the design brief, do some research.
2) There are loads of sources you could use to gain information:

Sources of information

books and fashion magazines   analysing existing products

the Internet, e.g. manufacturers' websites   surveys of shoppers

visiting museums and exhibitions   phone apps

The point of research is to:
1) Check that people will actually want your product.
2) Find out what similar products are on sale, and what people like and dislike about them.
3) Find out what materials and techniques would be suitable for making your product.
4) Find out how much the product is likely to cost to make, and how much you think it will sell for.

Now tell me about your design — but keep it brief...

The clue is in the name — design briefs don't need to be very long. They're just a starting point that highlights the key facts about what the designer needs to make, which will help them carry out any research.

Inspiration For Design

Every great new design starts with a great idea — the inspiration that gets the creative juices flowing. There are heaps of ways in which designers can come up with ideas for new creations.

Designers Come Up with New Ideas for Products

1) Designers are employed by manufacturers to come up with ideas for products in response to:

   - New innovations in technology (see page 4)
   - Gaps in the existing product range
   - Competition from rival manufacturers' products

2) The manufacturer starts by giving the designer a design brief (see page 1).

Designers Generate Ideas with a Variety of Methods

1) Making an ideas board by quickly coming up with lots of different ideas, in a group or individually.
2) Finding out about current trends by looking at magazines and websites, and visiting exhibitions.
3) Disassembling (taking apart) similar products to find out how they are made (see page 4).

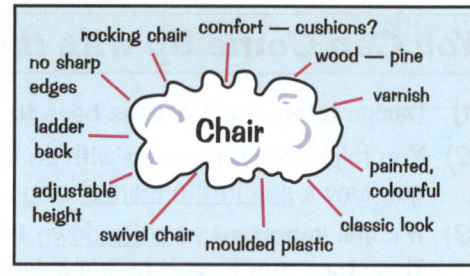

An example of an ideas board

A mood board

4) Creating mood boards — sticking a collection of photographs, colours and materials onto a big piece of paper to show the aesthetics (visuals, feel etc.) wanted for the product.
5) Talking to consumers, to find out what they like in that type of product (see page 7).
6) Adapting and extending existing products, e.g. creating a new look for a coffee table by using a different finish.

Creativity is Important in Design

1) Products that are innovative (new, different) will appeal to consumers and sell better than products that aren't.
2) It's important to evaluate products with this in mind — will it provide the same service or features as a hundred other products on the market? Or does it stand out by being different?

   Example — you could make your product more innovative by...
   - changing the shape
   - adding decoration
   - adapting a current design
   - combining materials or ingredients
   - combining features
   - filling a gap in the market

Boring Radios Ltd. — stereo-typical results guaranteed...

Don't be a boring radio designer — innovate, let your mind wander and avoid stereotypical responses.

Section 1 — Research and Analysis

Inspiration For Design

You Can Get *Inspiration* from *Patterns*...

1) Patterns using grids and repeating shapes are often used in product design. For example, fabrics often have a repeating pattern.
2) Many products, especially packaging, are based on simple geometric shapes such as squares, rectangles, circles and triangles.

...or *Nature*

Nature can be a design inspiration for the structure, function or aesthetics (look) of a product. When human creations copy designs from nature, it's called biomimicry.

Structure

1) The domes at the Eden Project are a very strong, lightweight structure, just like a honeycomb.

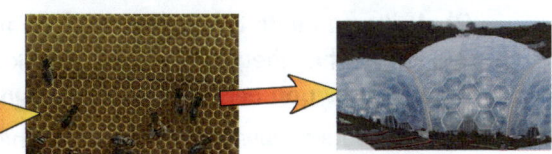

A honeycomb → The Eden Project

Function

1) Velcro® was invented by Swiss inventor George de Mestral after he noticed burs sticking to his clothes and his dog's fur.
2) After examining them under a microscope, he noticed tiny hooks that he could copy and use in his own design.

A bur sticking to fabric → Sticky shoe straps

Aesthetics

1) In baking, ingredients are often arranged to look like a natural structure.
2) Carrot cakes sometimes have sugar carrots on top, and pastries can be made to look like different flowers.

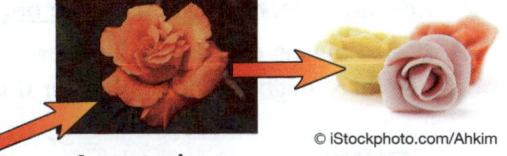

An actual rose → Pastry roses

Ergonomics Means Making the *Product Fit the User*

1) People come in all shapes and sizes, so most products need to vary to fit the user — this is known as ergonomics.
2) It can be important to design products ergonomically for health reasons, e.g. badly-designed shoes may damage your feet, ankles and knees if worn for long periods of time.
3) Some people might struggle with certain things — for example, children find buttons difficult, so their clothes are more likely to have large toggles or Velcro®.
4) User-centred design is a method of design that focuses on the needs of the people who will use the product (see page 6).

My inspiration for this joke was a little lacking, sorry...

It makes sense — not everyone works in the same way, so there are bound to be loads of approaches to designing. There are plenty of ways to get inspiration too, so make sure to always keep an eye out.

Section 1 — Research and Analysis

Analysing Products and Technology

It's not copying just because you looked at somebody else's work — lots of the best designs were just adaptations of previous products. It's important to look at what else is on the market, and how it works.

Product Analysis Can Give You Ideas For Your Design

1) If you need an idea for a product, you can use product analysis to see what's already on the market and what's not (gaps in the market).
2) Once you've got your design brief (see page 1) you can analyse a variety of similar products to help you with your own design.

If you wanted to design a reusable shopping bag, you could start by looking at ones that are already on the market.

Product Analysis Can Help You Understand a Product

1) During product analysis you should look carefully at the outside of the product, as well as taking it apart and looking at what's going on inside.
2) If it was made by professionals in any given industry, it's likely they knew what they were doing. Think about why they made it this way, and how you can apply their design and techniques to your own product.
3) You could draw inspiration from the products and techniques of past and present producers.

E.g. an old, handcrafted wooden toy train is very different to a modern, bright plastic toy train. You should ask yourself — what are their similarities and differences? What are the pros and cons of using the different materials? Look at how they've been made — what are the advantages and disadvantages of using each technique? Are the differences down to advancing technology, or are there other factors involved (e.g. changing trends)?

New Technology Impacts Designs

1) When coming up with new design ideas, you also need to look at current and emerging technology.
2) Advancing technology can make products viable that would have been too expensive or big before.
3) It also means certain products are no longer needed — your design idea could be great, but there might be no market for it because it uses old technology.

EXAMPLE: memory cards are getting smaller and cheaper

1) In the year 2000, memory cards were pretty big — around 4.5 cm tall, and you usually needed a special device just to read them.
2) A 128 MB model would set you back in the region of a whopping £200.
3) Nowadays you can fit gigabytes of storage in less than the space of a finger nail. What's more, it'll cost you less than 20 quid.
4) Say you wanted a way of easily showing off your photo collection — 15 years ago you could have designed a fold-out photo album that displayed your work beautifully without needing expensive storage or a display screen.
5) Now though, there isn't as much demand for a photo album because people can carry their entire photo collection on a single memory card. What's more, other technology such as tablet and laptop computers makes displaying the photos on the go quick and easy.

Product analysis of this book — it's awesome...

There you have it — it's important to always keep track of what other people are making, and what the latest advances in technology are. Spending a little time on your research could save you days in the long run.

Section 1 — Research and Analysis

Research and the Internet

The Internet, or Interned as my grandad calls it (he thinks its sole use is to connect people called Ned), can be the fastest, most useful research tool you've got, but there's a lot of rubbish to wade through.

Using the Internet is a Good Method of Research

1) Use the Internet to find information about materials and processes, and inspiration for designs — try looking at the websites of manufacturers, museums and D&T educational organisations.
2) You should be critical of the information you find though. Anyone can put information on the Internet — there's no guarantee that it's accurate.
3) Be careful of websites that seem biased (only give one side of an argument) or that don't give any evidence to back up what they say.

> If you find some interesting information on a website, check that the information is accurate before you use it in your work.
>
> Do more research to see if you can find information that confirms the facts on the website. Look in books or other websites.
>
> Do a second search to find out about the author of the website to see if they're a reliable source.

4) Give the source of your information when you're writing up your project, e.g. if you use our website then note down that the information came from www.cgpbooks.co.uk.
5) Remember that quality is important. Don't use every piece of information you find on the Internet. Read the information and if it's not relevant leave it out.

Contact Experts to Request Information

1) Experts are available on almost any subject. People who work in local industry will know a lot about designing and manufacturing products. Try contacting them by e-mail, forums or social media.
2) Be specific about what you want to find out, and be polite. Most people will help if they can.
3) E-mail contact details can usually be found on company websites, or you could try typing their name into a search engine.

It was digital. But not as they knew it.

Download Images from the Internet or Use a Device

1) You can save images from the Internet on your computer (this is called downloading images).
2) You could also upload your own images from a digital camera or smartphone. Some devices let you do this wirelessly, e.g. through Wi-Fi™ or Bluetooth®.
3) You can use a scanner to transfer ordinary pictures onto your computer and store them as digital images.
4) Mood boards (see page 2) are collections of images and colours that show the style you want for a product. You can create one on a computer using digital images.

You could also transfer ordinary pictures by taking a digital photo and uploading it.

smartphone

smart phone

The Internet — a big bundle of fun you can still call work...

With search engines getting better and better, and connections getting faster all the time, the Internet is a fantastic research tool. Just remember, not everything on the Internet is reliable — use your common sense.

Section 1 — Research and Analysis

Understanding Needs

Once you've identified your target group (p. 7), you also need to think about their specific needs. The disabilities, culture or religion of users may have an impact on how you design a product.

Products Need to be Accessible to Everyone

Lots of products are specifically designed to help people with disabilities.

1) Some packaging (e.g. for medication) has Braille labelling to give blind people information.
2) Control buttons can be made brightly coloured and extra large, so they're easy to find and press. For example, telephones, TV remotes and calculators can be made with big buttons.
3) Products such as smoke alarms can be designed with visible signals as well as audible ones so that deaf people can be alerted to fires.
4) Instructions can be given in picture or diagram form so that people who have difficulty reading text can still use the product.
5) Designers also have to think about wheelchair users. For example, trains and buses need to be designed to have wheelchair access.

Some people will find it easier to use a calculator with bigger buttons.

People Have Different Cultural and Religious Values

Designers need to cater for people with different customs and beliefs.

1) Some groups of people have different dietary needs. For example, Muslims only eat Halal foods and Jewish people only eat Kosher foods. Neither of these groups eat pork. 
2) Different groups have customs that focus on certain products. For example, the Hindu festival of Diwali is associated with lights.
3) Different cultures have different ways of doing things. For example, Japanese people traditionally eat at a low table sitting on the floor.
4) Clothing styles vary in different cultures.
5) Colours can have meanings, e.g. in China red is thought to be lucky.

Designers Need to Think About Age Groups

1) People in different age groups have different physical limitations.
2) Small children and elderly people may not be able to use small parts and might struggle undoing fastenings and opening packaging. Small parts could also be a choking hazard for children.
3) Elderly people might have difficulty holding and using products. Designers can think about putting large, easy-to-grip handles on, say, cutlery.
4) Age groups also need to be considered in the looks of a product. Adults might not want something that's too brightly coloured and childish.

The 'fuzzy panda keyring' — suitable for all ages.

Things we need — accessibility, ease of use, bread...

That pun's so bad I'm not sure I get it myself... but that's beyond the point — this page is full of super useful information for you to learn. Always remember to identify people's needs and make sure your product is accessible to as many people as possible. As well as being nice, it also means you'll sell more — win win.

Section 1 — Research and Analysis

Targeted Research

There's no use asking only adults about your product if it's aimed at children. Makes sense, right?

Identify Your Target Group and Ask Them Questions

Your target group is the group of people that you think will use your product, e.g. motor-heads, businessmen, middle-aged women, etc. Once you've worked out your target group, you can ask them questions directly. Here are some things you should try and find out:

1) Some information about the person — make sure they're in your target group.
2) Do they already buy the kind of product you're thinking of developing?
3) Do they like a particular style, colour or flavour?
4) How much would they be prepared to pay for this kind of product?
5) Where would they expect to buy it? (E.g. posh boutiques or cheap retailers).
6) Is there something they'd like from the product that existing products don't have?

Beth's target group had lots of opinions about what type of banana milkshake she should design...

You could present these questions in a:

Questionnaire — a form for people to fill in. Questions can be:

Closed questions — these have a limited number of possible answers, e.g. "do you prefer red or blue?".
Open questions — these have no set answers and allow for detail, e.g. "what's your favourite colour?".

Interview — a face to face conversation.

In interviews, you can start with the same sorts of questions as in questionnaires — but then take the chance to ask follow-up questions, based on the answers. This will help you get extra information and ideas by asking them to explain their answers, e.g. "why do you prefer blue shoes to red?".

Use Your Research to Draw Conclusions...

Once you've done some product analysis (page 4) and market research (see above), you should have loads of information. Now you have to use the information to help with your design:

1) Summarise what you've found out — pick out the most important and useful findings. It's good to try and find out what result(s) were most popular and why.

   Example
   Most children said they prefer red shoes because they are brightly coloured.

2) Explain what impact each finding will have on your design.

   Example
   Any shoes I make that are aimed at children should be brightly coloured.
   Red was the most popular colour, so it would be a good colour to use in the design.

Once you've done this, you can use your research to work out a list of conditions your design should meet. This is called a design specification — see page 10.

Targeted research — aim for the bullseye...

It's all well and good asking lots of intelligent questions, but if you're asking them to a bunch of chimps then you're unlikely to get any useful information. Unless you're asking about bananas, in which case — jackpot.

Section 1 — Research and Analysis

New Products and Technologies

People like to buy the latest gadgets — like wireless headphones or a top of the range tablet computer. There's always new stuff on the market to make you think, "Ooooh, I definitely need one of those".

There are Lots of New Products on the Market

1) There is consumer demand for new and improved products.
   This is called "market pull" — manufacturers produce what people want to buy.
2) Advances in technology mean that new products can be designed, e.g. smartphones and GPS watches.
3) Re-styled versions of existing products are produced to keep up with fashion.
   Appearance has a huge part to play in what consumers will and won't buy.
4) Manufacturers are in competition with each other to get consumers to buy their products.
   Producing new and improved products is a way of keeping consumers loyal to their brand.

Some Products Fail or are Replaced Regularly

Some products fail because they're rubbish.

1) Some products aren't marketed successfully — so consumers aren't aware of the product and what's good about it.
2) Sometimes another, similar product is available which is cheaper or more stylish, so consumers buy that instead.
3) Advances in technology mean that products become outdated (see page 4).

Use Criteria to Evaluate and Compare New Products

These are the criteria (standards) you should use to compare and evaluate new products:
1) FUNCTION/USEFULNESS — Does the product do its job well?
2) AESTHETICS — Does the product look and feel good? Is it fashionable?
3) AFFORDABILITY — Is the product affordable for the target customers?
4) PROFITABILITY — Are manufacturing costs low enough to make a profit?
5) HEALTH AND SAFETY — Are there any hazards in using the product, e.g. sharp edges?
6) UNIQUE FEATURES — Does the product have any special features which its rivals don't have?

New Products and Technologies Impact Many Things

Evolving technology has an impact on a number of things, from the way we communicate and develop designs to the way we dispose of them.

1) COMMUNICATION — ICT allows us to communicate instantly with people around the world (see next page). This means it's easy to spread news about new products, but difficult to keep them a secret from rivals before they're finished. So somebody might copy you and release their own version first.
2) THE ENVIRONMENT — Because technology is rapidly evolving, new products are constantly bought to replace old ones. E.g. old mobile phone handsets need to be disposed of responsibly so that they won't damage the environment. The materials and processes used also need to be considered (p. 28-29).
3) SOCIETY — Technology affects the way people interact with each other — new products can spark new trends, or completely replace the old ways of doing things (more on the next page).

A new mobile with jet pack and ejector seat — I need it...

I'm sure you'll know the feeling — everyone always wants the newest and flashiest product on the market. Just learn how that affects and is affected by all the things above — there's a lot of information here.

Section 1 — Research and Analysis

The Impact of Technology

Communication systems are everywhere — radio, TV, mobiles, e-mail and social media mean you can access and communicate information easily and quickly. This has changed the way people live and work.

Technology Means a Team Can Work in Different Places

1) The people designing a product no longer have to work in the same area, e.g. a design team can work in different places and use the Internet to exchange design ideas. This is called remote working.
2) Remote working is possible because advances in technology have improved communication systems. The Internet lets us send text, images, videos and data around the world very quickly.
3) Video-conferencing allows people to have long-distance meetings. A camera can be connected to most computers, but many new devices have one built-in. People can see and speak to each other in real time, and several people can be connected this way.
4) People can also communicate indirectly by posting ideas on Internet messaging boards or commenting on others' ideas. This means many people can work on the same idea without meeting up in real life.

Advantages of remote working

1) Remote working is good for designers because it means they can work for a broader range of clients and on a broader range of projects.
2) Remote working is good for manufacturers because it means they can use the best designers available, worldwide.
3) It allows home-working and flexible hours for workers who want it.
4) It saves on transport costs and pollution.

Disadvantages of remote working

1) It takes more effort to coordinate a team working in different areas.
2) Some people may prefer a more sociable working environment.
3) Coming up with ideas and developing them as a team is often easier face to face.

Technology has an Impact on Individuals and Society

Computers are used in shops, homes, schools, offices, banks, cars, fridges... They're everywhere — and they affect the way people live.

1) Some people are critical of the effect technology has on society. They argue that new technology increases the pace of life and makes it more stressful.
2) Prolonged use of a computer and keyboard can cause health problems, e.g. Repetitive Strain Injury (RSI), or reduce the amount of exercise people do. Designers of computer office equipment need to consider this kind of thing when they're coming up with new products.
3) Other people argue that technology has a positive impact on society. It means it's easier for people to connect and communicate ideas, or form organisations internationally.
4) This is extra useful if you're interested in designing or finding out more about an obscure or rare product — it's easy to find a group of people who are also interested in doing the same.
5) The Internet has oodles of information. People can publish reviews on various websites at the click of a button, so you'll get tons of feedback and free advertising. On the other hand, people can also write bad reviews, so you can't flog a dodgy product and get away with it. Also beware when you're reading reviews — people can say whatever they want so the reviews might not always be honest and unbiased.

MAN

The year 2105

I can't get this remote working — the TV won't turn on...

There you have it — where would you be without the Internet? Well, the '80s probably...

Section 1 — Research and Analysis

Section 2 — Development and Evaluation

Design Specifications

So, you've got a design brief and a great wodge of research. Time to start writing a design specification...

A Design Specification is a List of Product Features

1) Once you've got your design brief and done your research, you need to use them to draw up a list of features (design criteria) the product you're designing should have. This list is called a design specification.

2) When you're writing up the design specification think about how the finished product will affect the target consumers.

Questions to ask when writing a design specification
- How can you ensure it matches the design brief?
- Can you make the product safe, so it won't harm the consumers?
- Can you make the product cheap enough for the consumers to afford?
- What shapes, textures, colours and flavours will the consumers prefer?

FEATURES
cute, hairy, difficult to peel

3) Here's an example of a design specification for balaclavas:

Function — The product should be a warm balaclava, suitable for cold weather.
Cost — Each balaclava should cost no more than £4 to make.
Aesthetics — The product should have a soft texture, so it's comfortable to wear. It should look stylish.
Manufacture — The product should be fairly easy to manufacture, and take no more than 2 hours to make.
The Environment — Care must be taken that the materials and packaging are environmentally friendly.
Health and Safety — The product shouldn't restrict the wearer's ability to see.

Next you Need to Produce Some Ideas

1) First, think up key words and questions about your product. Use the design specification to guide you.
2) Let your imagination run wild. Even if an idea sounds ridiculous, put it down anyway. Be creative and get as many ideas down as you can that match your design specification.
3) You might want to combine the best features from a few of your ideas to generate a really good idea.
4) Choose the design which fits the design specification best.

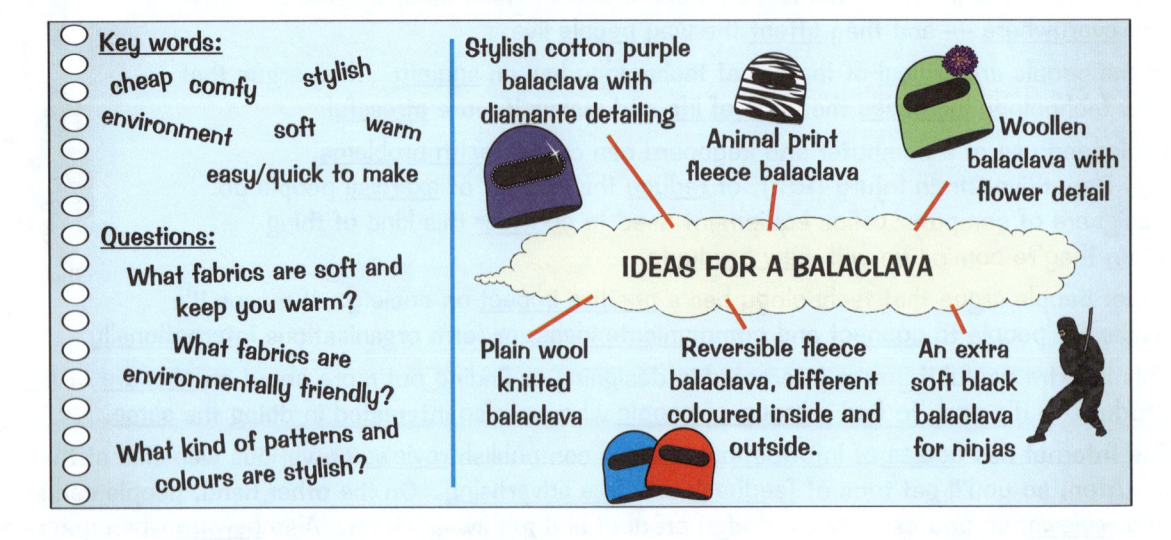

Key words:
cheap comfy stylish
environment soft warm
easy/quick to make

Questions:
What fabrics are soft and keep you warm?
What fabrics are environmentally friendly?
What kind of patterns and colours are stylish?

IDEAS FOR A BALACLAVA

Stylish cotton purple balaclava with diamante detailing

Animal print fleece balaclava

Woollen balaclava with flower detail

Plain wool knitted balaclava

Reversible fleece balaclava, different coloured inside and outside.

An extra soft black balaclava for ninjas

I made a balaclava once — I overdid it on the almonds...

You need to think your design through carefully (making sure it's affordable, marketable, attractive and useful) because otherwise your product will be pants — the sort that people don't buy.

Section 2 — Development and Evaluation

Planning

Once you've decided on the design for your product, you need to plan your method for making it.

Choosing Materials — You Need the Right Properties

Choose materials or ingredients with properties that are suitable for your design. You must be able to give reasons for the materials or ingredients you choose. Good questions to ask yourself include:

1) Strength — can it withstand the forces on it without breaking?
2) Workability — can it be shaped, cut and joined without cracking or breaking?
3) Durability — will it withstand wear and tear?
4) Flavour and texture — will the flavour and texture of an ingredient work together with other ingredients to make a good dish?
5) Cost — is it affordable?
6) Aesthetics — does it look and feel right for the product/market?
7) Availability — is it available to buy locally?

Manufacturing Specifications — How to Make Your Product

Your manufacturing specification must explain the design, materials and method for making your product. Include enough information for somebody else to make your product. Include all this stuff:

1) Details of the processes that will be used to put the product together.
2) A list of the materials or ingredients that will make up the product.
3) Measurements — the sizes and weights of each part of the product.
4) Tolerances — the maximum and minimum variations from the standard size or weight.
5) Finish — e.g. how the materials are protected and what the required colours are.
6) Quality control — the checks needed to make sure the product fits together and works.
7) Costing — the cost of materials or ingredients, tools, machinery and workers' time.

Plan the Order and Timing of Producing the Product

Predict how much time will be needed to carry out each stage of production.
1) Use tables or flow charts to represent the production process (see page 19).
2) Show every stage of the process in order.
3) Gantt charts are time plans, drawn out in sequence.
   Use one to show how long each stage will take for your product.

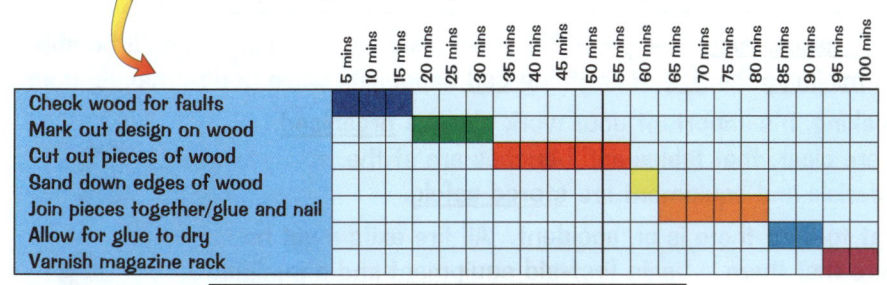

A Gantt chart for making a magazine rack

Dave didn't really understand Gantt charts...

Decisions decisions...

Choosing the right materials or ingredients can be tricky — you'll normally have lots of choice. Make sure you use your design specification to help decide which ones are going to give you the best product in the end.

Section 2 — Development and Evaluation

Planning

Go with the flow, man... and by flow, I mean a detailed flow chart of exactly how to make your product.

Use Flow Charts to Show the Order of Tasks

1) A flow chart gives a great overview of the whole process, so include one in your manufacturing specification.
2) It shows what tasks need to be done when.
3) It also includes checks at various stages to ensure consistency and quality.

See page 19 for more on flow charts.

Decisions go in diamond-shaped boxes. These let you show where quality should be checked.

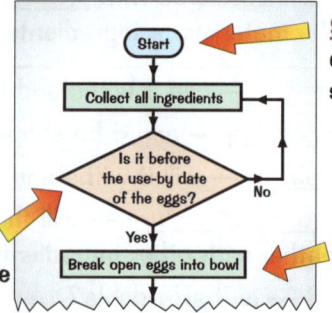

Start and end a flow chart with a sausage-shaped box.

Processes go in rectangular boxes.

Compromise and Prioritise when Planning

When choosing materials and production techniques, you need to work out your priorities. Strike a balance between these factors:

1) Cost — your product needs to be the right price for your market.
2) Appropriate materials, tools and processes — the quality needs to be high enough for your market.
3) Time — there's always a deadline or time limit on how long you can take to make your product.

Example 1 — A toy slingshot

Design specification: The toy needs to be cheap, but the slingshot handle needs to be light and strong. Making a slingshot handle from fibreglass would make it light and strong, but fibreglass is expensive. Instead it would be better to make it from PVC, which is still strong and light, but much cheaper.

Example 2 — Making lasagne for 30 people

Design specification: The lasagne needs to be home made, use quality ingredients and serve 30 people. The food must take no more than 4 hours to make.
Making fresh pasta for this many people in under 4 hours is a tall order — instead you could use shop-bought pasta sheets but make the sauces from scratch with top quality ingredients — that way you save loads of time and the difference might not even be noticeable.

Think about Health and Safety when Planning

1) You should carry out a risk assessment (see page 27) when planning. That way, you'll be able to spot any possible hazards and minimise the risk of anything bad happening while you're making your product.
2) No matter what you're making, it's important your work place is organised. Check that all walkways are clear, that tables and benches are at the right height, and that materials and equipment are stored safely.
3) Make sure you know what to do if there is an accident. All fire exits must be marked clearly. Make sure that there is basic first-aid equipment and a qualified first-aider around. Find out how to turn off machines quickly in an emergency.

Pailing to flan is flanning to pail...

Planning is dead important, even if it feels like the most boring thing ever. If you don't do it, you're bound to get half way through and realise you've made a great big howler, by which time it's too late.

Section 2 — Development and Evaluation

Modelling

So, you've picked the idea you want to develop. Now it's time to get into the details and come up with a model to see what works best for your design before going to production and making a whole load of them.

Use Detailed Sketches and Maths to Help you Design

1) Your first sketches of your product should be rough, freehand pencil drawings.
2) The next stage is to make some more detailed drawings.
3) It helps you to see what will actually work in practice and it might help you decide on details you hadn't thought about before, e.g. the sizes or positions of components or how parts should be constructed and fitted together.
4) It might also be useful to do a bit of maths to help you with your design. For example, say you're making a bucket that has to be able to hold a volume of 1 litre of water. You could use formulas to work out the possible dimensions your product could have based on its shape. With a little technical know-how, you could also use a computer program to show this info on a graph. This is called mathematical modelling.

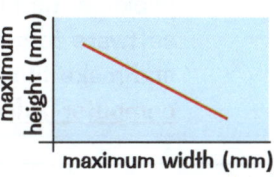

Create a Model or Prototype

1) Once you've got your detailed sketches and maths done, it's a good idea to make a prototype (a model) of your design. The prototype you make depends on your product and what you want to test. For example, your prototype could be:

- A scaled-down version of your design.
- A full-size version of your design but made using cheap materials.
- A one-off version of your design made using the right materials or ingredients before the product is mass produced (see page 18).

The ratio 1:10 is the easiest scale to use when making a scale model. (You just move the decimal point on your measurements by one place).

2) 3D models are a great way of finding out whether your design will work.
3) A prototype can allow you to see the final design in 3D without wasting money on lots of materials or ingredients. E.g. you can make up a clothes pattern using newspaper to check that all the pieces fit together.
4) Producing a prototype can help you find out which shapes, colours and materials will suit your design best.
5) Making prototypes also helps show up any problems — see next page.
6) It is common in industry for lots of prototypes to be made, not just the one.

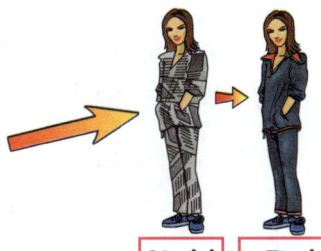

Virtual Models can be Really Useful

1) Designing a product using a computer is (unsurprisingly) called computer-aided design (CAD).
2) You can use 3D modelling software like Autodesk Inventor® to create a virtual model of your product. The model looks 3D and can be rotated through 360°.
3) As long as you know what you're doing, models can be made quicker, cheaper and more accurately using computers.
4) You can do a range of tests on a computer model so you can iron out mistakes before you spend time and money making a physical model.

RIA NOVOSTI/SCIENCE PHOTO LIBRARY

Modelling can be tough, but don't pout...

What ever you're designing, it's important to make a model to work out if your product is the masterpiece it is in your head. If you don't make a model, a design mistake could be a very expensive mistake.

Section 2 — Development and Evaluation

Modelling

Once you've made a prototype, you can test it and use it to improve your design to make it the bestest.

You can Make Prototypes by Hand or Using CAD/CAM

1) The simplest way to make a prototype is just to make it by hand, especially if it's a food product.
2) If you've made your design using a CAD package, you may be able to get the computer software to connect to a processing machine and make the prototype. This is called computer-aided manufacture (CAM) (see p.23).

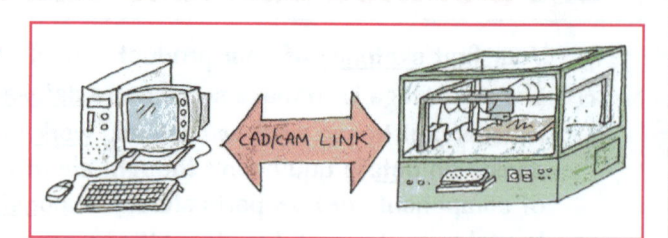

Use Modelling to Spot Problems with Your Design

1) Modelling is a good way to spot (and solve) problems with your design.
2) Try out different aspects of your design. For example, you could model just one part of the product separately, to check it works, before going on to the rest.
3) Modelling can also help you spot issues in the way you make your product. E.g. when making your model it might become obvious that decorating your product the way you planned would take too long, or that there is a better way of doing it. You can use this information to adapt your design and manufacturing specification.

Not that kind...

You Need to Test, Evaluate and Improve Each Prototype

1) For a prototype to be useful, you really need to test it to check that it's how it should be.
2) You might find there are some things that don't work out quite how you'd hoped.
3) You could make several prototypes that are each slightly different and test them all. For example, you could make basic cookies but add different flavourings to each cookie. You could then test them by getting people to rate them on which ones look best, taste best etc.
4) Use the results of your testing to improve your design and make another version of your prototype.

- If there's a problem, suggest how to fix it and try out another version of the model.
- See if you can combine good features from a few prototypes to make an even better one.

5) Record how the design develops — take photos of your models.
6) You should also evaluate each model against the design specification (see page 10). Take each point on the specification and see if your model is up to scratch.

Iterative Design Means Testing a Prototype Over and Over

Iterative design is the name given to a process in which you continually test and improve a single prototype, until you have created a design that you're happy with.

1) Design and create a prototype.
2) Test your prototype out on your target group.
3) Use feedback from your target group to improve the prototype.
4) Test the improved prototype on your target group.
5) Keep repeating this process — redesign, test and improve your prototype until you've got the perfect design.

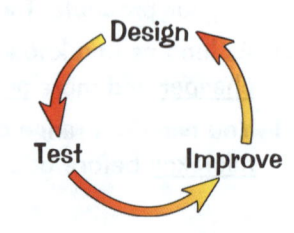

Test your product on the catwalk...

Testing out design ideas is really important. They might look great on paper, but when it comes to making them they might be totally impractical. And, while you're at it, why not evaluate them too?

Section 2 — Development and Evaluation

Presenting Ideas

Once designers are completely satisfied with a design, they write a report (see next page) and present the idea to the client. The client can then decide whether it's what they want.

You Might Need to Present Your Final Design

It's important to present your design clearly and with as big an impact as possible. The best way to do this is with really good presentation drawings — they help the client to clearly visualise the product.

1) You should ideally have two different types of presentation drawing:

- A working drawing with dimensions and other details, e.g. materials and finishes. The client will probably want to see this one too — and the manufacturer definitely needs it.
- A 3D drawing showing how the finished product will look. This could include pictures of the product in use or in its environment.

2) Presentation drawings can be done using CAD (see page 13). You can make 3D drawings look very realistic by adding texture and light effects. And if you do working drawings in CAD, they'll be very neat and accurate.

3) Neat, hand-drawn presentation drawings are also fine. The downside of doing this in industry is that the designer would have to re-draw it if the client wanted them to make any alterations.

4) It's important to annotate your drawings to show how your product meets the design specification. You could also include a really short description of the product and its best features to help explain the drawings.

Use Tables and Charts to Present Your Findings

1) When making a presentation, it can be really useful to put information from your research, e.g. survey results, into a table or chart to make it easy to understand.

2) This then makes it easier for you to show how you've used the data to support the decisions you've made for your final design.

3) You can use a spreadsheet program to display data and do calculations to analyse your results.

4) If you put your data in a spreadsheet, you should easily be able to come up with clear charts and graphs to show in your presentation.

	A	B
1	Material	£ per sq. metre
2	Copper	69
3	Cardboard	1.5
4	Thermoplastic	20
5	Plywood	6
6	Pine	15

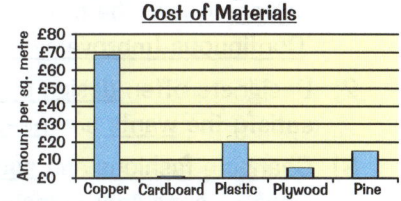

You May Need to Give an Oral Presentation

You might need to give an oral presentation (a talk) on your design and explain what its key features are, who the product is aimed at, why you've decided on this particular design etc.

1) Just keep calm and make sure you cover all the points you want to make about your product. It can be really helpful to use note cards with the key points you want to cover on them as prompts.

2) You might get asked questions — have a think what you might get asked and how you will answer before your talk.

3) You can use software such as Microsoft® PowerPoint® to make digital presentations. You can use it to make slides that show the key points of your talk. The slides can display any digital sketches, models, charts, data etc.

Bad ideas can look great, good ideas can look rubbish...

...it's all in the presentation — so make sure you prepare well and your presentations are spot on.

Section 2 — Development and Evaluation

Evaluating and Adapting Designs

So, you've tested, re-tested and you think you've got the best product you can make. What's next?

Evaluate Your Final Design in a Written Report

Want to know if your design's a winner? It's evaluation time.

1) The point of evaluating your design is to identify its good and bad points and make sure it does everything you need it to.
2) Write your evaluation up as a report. You could include:

> - Whether it satisfies all the points of your design brief and design specification.
> - A description and any sketches or photos you have of your prototypes.
> - The results of prototype testing (how it looks, smells, feels or tastes).
> - The comments of people in your target group.
> - Description of any changes you've made to your design and why you made them.
> - A detailed description and pictures of your final design.
> - An accurate manufacturing specification which takes into account any changes that have happened to the design during its development.
> - Any ways you can think of improving the product in the future which you've not been able to do due to cost, time, not the right machinery etc.
> - A discussion on whether your timings are still accurate after other changes are taken into account.

Products Evolve and Get Improved Over Time

Once you've got your final product made, it doesn't mean you're done and dusted. Products are always changing — this is known as product evolution, and there are lots of reasons for it.

1) Manufacturers are always looking for ways to make more money. One way to do this is by improving how they make their products, e.g. improving the design so that the product can be made more easily and cheaply. This is called 'Continuous Improvement'. It's a big reason why products evolve.
2) Designers often design stuff (and manufacturers make it) to satisfy the wants and needs of consumers — consumer demand.
3) Changing fashions and social attitudes affect the kind of products people want — consumer demand won't always be for the same things or styles.
4) Technology is always changing, so something that wasn't possible ten years ago might now be used to make a product better. Customers also often want the latest version of a product with all the fancy gadgets and gizmos, e.g. mobile phones.

> When mobile phones first came out they were fairly big and bulky and could only be used to make phone calls. As technology improved, mobile phones got smaller and phones started to be able to connect to the Internet. Nowadays, it's easy to get a touchscreen phone with a fast Internet connection, access to hundreds of apps, video calling etc.

5) So designers have to adapt their designs to match the changing wants and needs of consumers.

Don't write on an empty stomach — use paper...

Evaluating and adapting is never over for a designer. Your product can be perfect when you design it, but if people decide in a year they want a jazzier version, you'll need to adapt your product to keep it relevant.

Section 2 — Development and Evaluation

Product Evolution and Design Movements

Sometimes products are made or evolve because there's a need for something to help people.

Products Can Evolve to Fill a Need

Sometimes products evolve because there's a social or cultural need...

Example — Wind up radios

Trevor Baylis heard that educational radio broadcasts might help stop the spread of AIDS in Africa. But many rural areas didn't have electricity so couldn't use radios. So Baylis designed and made a wind-up radio that didn't need an electricity supply.

...or because there's a political or environmental need:

Example — Environmentally friendly products

Environmentally friendly products are popular now — many consumers are put off buying products that waste resources or can't be recycled. Designers have to take this into account with new products. For example, car manufacturers now aim to produce cars with improved fuel-efficiency.

Design Movements Influence Product Development

Designs come in and out of fashion, so products made in a particular style are often made around the same time. This is called a design movement. There are lots of exciting design movements you could use as an influence when designing a product. Here are just a few...

Art Nouveau designs are flowing and curvy. They often use floral or insect patterns. Well-known Art Nouveau designers are Louis C. Tiffany and René Lalique.

Art Deco was inspired by African and Egyptian art. It involves bold colours, geometric, zigzag and stepped shapes, bold sweeping curves and sunburst patterns. Examples of Art Deco architecture include the Chrysler Building in New York.

Bauhaus was a design movement in Germany founded by Walter Gropius. His motto was 'form follows function' — he thought that products should be designed with their function as the starting point, rather than their appearance. Furniture in the Bauhaus style often has chrome tubing and black leather.

Postmodernist designers rejected the 'form follows function' idea — they thought that style should be the starting point. The Memphis movement was at the height of postmodernism — a famous design is Ettore Sottsass's Carlton cabinet. Memphis designs used many bright, contrasting colours and different materials.

Nothing's ever good enough...

So designers often come up with new products because of public demand, or because there's new technology. But designers can also be inspired by previous design movements.

Section 2 — Development and Evaluation

Section 3 — Production and Industry

Scale of Production

The scale of production is how many items you make. Some products are made as one-offs — but they're expensive. Mass produced stuff is more affordable and often does the job nicely.

One-Off Production Suits Luxury Products

1) One-off production is also called jobbing production. One product is made at a time for an individual customer's needs.
2) The look and function of the product are tailored to the client.
3) One-off products are usually expensive. Production is very labour intensive (it takes a lot of time to produce a single product), and highly skilled workers are needed.
4) One-off production suits complex or luxury items, e.g. exhibition displays, hand-made furniture, fitted kitchens, oil rigs, satellites, wedding dresses and wedding cakes.

High-Volume Production = Lots of Identical Products

1) High-volume production is also called mass production. Products are manufactured in very large quantities and are usually cheaper than similar products made as one-offs.
2) Materials and components can be bought in bulk, which makes them cheaper.
3) This type of production often uses expensive, specialised equipment including Computer-Aided Manufacture (CAM) (see page 23) and industrial robots.
4) Production is often continuous — running 24 hours/day.
5) A large workforce is needed, but the work is usually less skilled than for one-off production.
6) Mass production suits products for which there is high demand and which need to be affordable to a wide range of people, e.g. cars, electrical plugs, biros, fridges and washing machines.

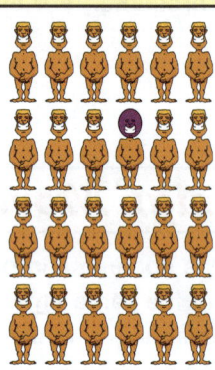

NEWSFLASH: Random-plum-head problem once again blights Nudeman factory.

Mass-Produced Goods are Cheaper

1) The cost of making a single item gets lower the greater the number that are manufactured — this is called economy of scale.
2) Large amounts of raw materials and components are needed for mass production. Manufacturers are able to negotiate discounts and lower prices for materials. This is called purchasing power.
3) Products are often mass-produced using a production line — where each worker does a single task repetitively. This is very quick and efficient — which saves money.

Pies eaten — mass produced (mainly in the belly region)...

The products you make in school will usually be by one-off production. Unless you really want to unleash 500 laminated, plywood keyrings on the world...

Batch Production

Heaven, I'm in heaven. And my heart beats so that I can hardly speak.
And I seem to find the happiness I seek. When I'm out batch producing... Darn, I'm such a geek.

Batch Production Makes a Group of Identical Products

1) A specific quantity ("batch") of identical products are produced at a time. More than one batch can be made of the same product, using the same materials and equipment.
2) The machinery used is adaptable. Changes can be made to the design of the product from batch to batch, e.g. a table can be made with different types of finish. The changes don't tend to be major — just variations on a theme.
3) The time between batches, when machines and tools may have to be set up differently or changed around, is called downtime. This is unproductive and needs to be kept short — so the manufacturer doesn't lose money.
4) The size of a batch can vary hugely — from twenty to twenty thousand.
5) Batch-produced products include aircraft, DVDs, books, clothing, radios and bread.

Flow Charts Show the Production Process

1) A flow chart is a simple diagram showing the order of production. It works just as well for a simple school project as for a complex manufacturing process.
2) There are standard symbols used in flow charts. The symbols are linked by arrows.
3) Feedback loops are put in at points where you need to make a decision about the quality of your product so far. If it's not good enough, you go back to an earlier stage in the process.
4) You can draw a flow chart to show a batch production process. Use a diamond-shaped decision box to show the places where you could vary the basic design of your product, e.g. colour, flavour, material, finish.

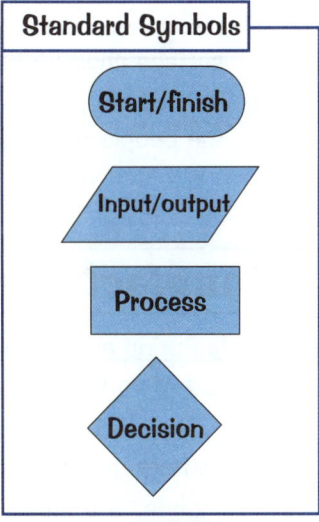

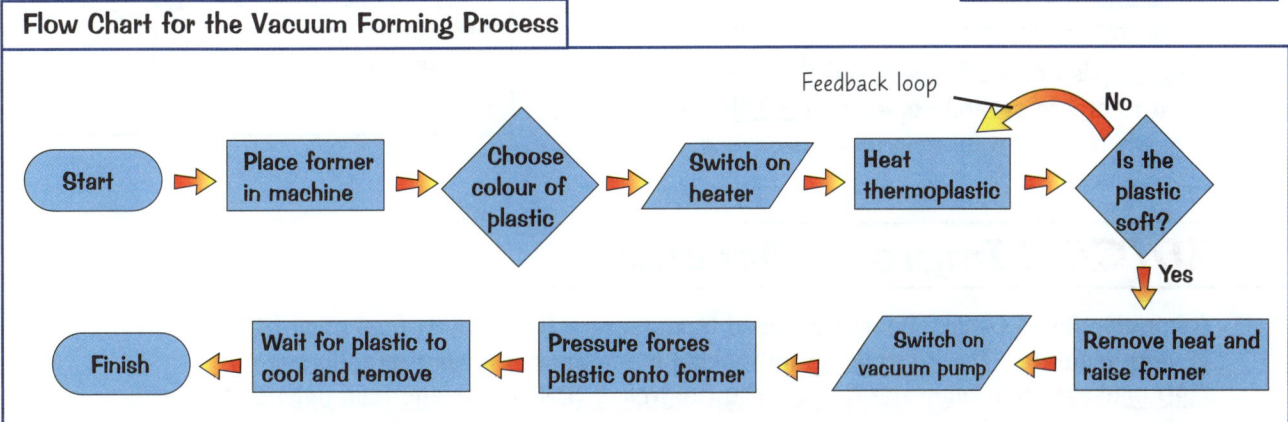

Standard Symbols
- Start/finish
- Input/output
- Process
- Decision

Flow Chart for the Vacuum Forming Process

Start → Place former in machine → Choose colour of plastic → Switch on heater → Heat thermoplastic → Is the plastic soft? (Feedback loop — No)

Yes → Remove heat and raise former → Switch on vacuum pump → Pressure forces plastic onto former → Wait for plastic to cool and remove → Finish

A batch — a cross between a bat and a chip...

Bonnie: "You should be ashamed, stealing old ladies' automobiles." Clyde: "Actually, I was thinking of buying me one." Bonnie: "Bull — you ain't got money for dinner, let alone buy no car."
Bonnie and Clyde discuss the Model T Ford — an early example of mass production.

Section 3 — Production and Industry

Quality and Accuracy

If you buy something that doesn't work, you can take it back and demand a refund.
So if manufacturers want to make money, they've got to make sure their products aren't cack.

Quality Control is Different from Quality Assurance

Quality Assurance

1) Quality Assurance (or QA) is all about standards — standards are set before a product is made to make sure that the final product comes out the way the manufacturer wants it to.
2) Standards cover everything from the quality of raw materials to the packaged product.
3) The manufacturer guarantees to the consumer that the product will be of sufficient quality.

Quality Control

1) Quality Control (or QC) happens on the product during, or after, it's been made. It's the checking process that goes on to make sure the Quality Assurance standards are met and the final product is up to scratch.
2) Quality Control involves inspection, sampling and testing.
3) There's usually a Quality Control Department in factories, which takes charge of all the testing and inspections.
4) Inspections are made for variations from the standard size, colour, and surface characteristics, and to make sure the product works properly.
5) Part of the system is feedback. If something isn't up to standard, then the people responsible are told so that they can fix the problem.

He knew the surface defect was out there — scared, lonely, ready to kill...

Manufacturing Aids Ensure Repetitive Quality

Manufacturing aids like jigs, moulds and templates ensure accuracy when producing a batch of identical products.

1) Jigs are used to position materials and give you a guide for where you should saw, drill and so on.
2) Templates are things you draw or cut around to get the same shape and size each time.
3) Moulds (also called formers and dies) can be used to create several copies of a 3D shape, e.g. when vacuum forming or sand-casting.

This jig fits over the end of the plank and makes it easy to drill the holes in the right places.

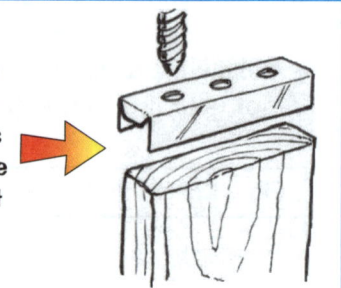

CAD/CAM Improves Accuracy

1) Computer-Aided Design/Computer-Aided Manufacture (CAD/CAM) (see page 14) is very accurate. The information for making a component is sent directly from a CAD package to a Computer Numerically Controlled (CNC) machine (see page 26).
2) The same information can be sent repetitively to the machine, guaranteeing identical results.
3) CAD/CAM is often used in industry to mass produce products.

Quality Street® — everyone's favourite soap about chocolates...
You need to use Quality Control on the products you make — stuff like checking that raw materials don't have flaws and testing the final product to make sure it works. If it don't work, it don't sell.

Section 3 — Production and Industry

Manufacturing and Processing

Making things on a large scale is risky — what if it goes wrong? That's why we test on a small scale first.

Test your Product on a Small Scale First

1) Before you start a large scale batch production process, you have to test the production of your product on a small scale.
2) Try out your ideas by making samples (sometimes called prototypes).
3) There are lots of advantages to making samples —

- They show whether the production process works.
- You don't waste money on large quantities of materials.
- You can find errors at an early stage.
- You can check your samples against the design specification and see how well they match up.

The Manufacturing Process can Limit Designs

Manufacturers have to think about how easy a design will be to make, e.g.

1) The shelf-life of a product — All natural products will eventually 'go off' and be unfit to eat. The shorter the shelf-life of a product, the less time there is to sell it in.
2) How long the product will take to make — The product needs to be produced quickly enough to reach the consumer while it can still be sold, e.g. clothing before it goes out of fashion, or food before it 'goes off'.
3) The cost and availability of ingredients — They need to be cheap enough for the completed product to still make a profit.
4) The cost of manufacture — Manufacturers need to take into account how much time and energy it takes to make the product. They have to consider staff costs, power costs and any special machinery needed.

Commercial Food Processing — Extending Shelf-Life

Food is made to stay fresh longer by either killing harmful bacteria or by slowing their growth. This can be done by using a number of processing techniques, e.g.

Heat Treatment

1) Pasteurisation uses heat to reduce the number of harmful bacteria in the food — this is short-term preservation.
2) Canning/bottling is where the food is cooked to kill all harmful bacteria. The food is then placed in a sterile (bacteria-free) container, which is vacuum-sealed (air is removed). This stops food coming into contact with the air or other sources of bacteria.

Chilling

1) Food is cooked quickly to kill bacteria and is then chilled until it is needed. This slows the growth of harmful bacteria that can cause food poisoning.
2) Freezing allows food to be stored for long periods as the bacteria stop growing while the food is frozen. The bacteria start to grow again when the food begins to thaw.

Do it like a fish painter — start on a small scale...

I've thought about how the design will affect manufacturing and I've made my prototype. I'm ready to go. Ladies and gentlemen, I give you 'flat-pat' furniture — tables and chairs made from cow dung. How ethical.

Section 3 — Production and Industry

Industry

Without the Industrial Revolution, most of us would still be out working in the fields. Isn't industry great? This page shows the different jobs in industry, the role of ICT and how industry's changed over time.

There are Many Different Jobs in Industry

1) Companies are made up of teams of people.
   - Managers are responsible for running departments within a company.
   - Supervisors give tasks to operators. Operators work machines.
   - Engineers design and build machinery to make products.
   - Maintenance staff install and repair machinery.
2) Three of the most important managerial positions are: design manager, production manager and marketing manager.

I tell you, these guys will work for peanuts.

Neep!

The Design Manager
1) Draws up the design criteria with the clients.
2) Oversees the designing process.
3) Oversees the production of the prototypes.
4) Decides on the final product specification.
5) Keeps in close contact with the production manager.

The Production Manager
1) Makes the prototype design ready for large-scale production.
2) Organises the manufacturing.
3) Organises the set-up and running of the machines.
4) Is responsible for quality control checks and safety checks.

The Marketing Manager
1) Makes sure there is a gap in the market for the new product.
2) Researches what customers want from the new product.
3) Develops the marketing campaign.

ICT is Important in the Manufacturing Industry

1) Computers can control industrial machinery, e.g. milling machines, ovens, lathes, presses.
2) Computers are also useful in industry because they speed up communication. Departments within an organisation can send each other information quickly and easily via e-mail.
3) The improvements in communications enable remote working, e.g. a designer can work in a different country to the manufacturer, but still send in their ideas quickly.

iStockphoto.com/Mark Bowden

There's more on ICT in industry on page 25.

Local Manufacturing has Changed Over Time

1) Many big companies have moved their production sites abroad, to areas where labour is cheaper. This means they employ fewer people in Britain.
2) Large companies manufacture products in high-volume, which keeps the price of the final products low. It's hard for smaller manufacturing firms to compete and stay in business.
3) Modern materials have changed the manufacturing industry. New products can be designed and manufactured, and some older products stop being produced.

ICT — a jumbled up, parasitic blood-sucker...

Computers can be used to do boring and repetitive work. Fortunately for you, school work is exciting and by no means repetitive. Now turn the page, read and absorb. Turn, read, absorb. Turn, read, absorb...

Section 3 — Production and Industry

Computer-Aided Manufacture

Computers are brilliant at lots of stuff, they don't take sick days and don't sneak an extra couple of minutes on a tea break. Nowadays, most products have been made with the help of a computer...

CAM — Computer-Aided Manufacture

1) Computer-Aided Manufacture (CAM) means the process of manufacturing products with the help of computers.
2) CAM is linked to CAD (page 14). Products are designed with CAD software. Then data from the CAD software is downloaded into the control unit of a manufacturing machine which makes each component or product.
3) The machines used in CAM are Computer Numerically Controlled (CNC) — see page 26.

Products manufactured using CAD/CAM

CAM is Great for Mass Production

CAM is really useful in mass production (see page 18). Computer-controlled machines are used as part of the production line — to do repetitive tasks to a reliable standard of accuracy.

Advantages of CAM

1) CAM makes production quicker and more efficient. Machines do not need to rest, so productivity is increased. This means manufacturers can respond quickly to demand for a product and can make more profit.
2) CAM is very accurate — there's less chance of human error.
3) It can be used to process materials and chemicals which are hazardous to humans.
4) It can be used for repetitive tasks that workers would find boring.
5) CAM is good for batch production (page 19). New instructions can be downloaded and programmed into a machine quickly and easily. So batches of slightly different products can be produced using the same machinery.

Dylan was glad that the computers were taking over the snail soup production process.

But there are Disadvantages

The disadvantages of CAM are similar to those of CAD:
1) The initial cost of the computer hardware and software and CNC machines is high.
2) Training programmers and operators is expensive.
3) The use of computers and automated machines means fewer workers (and fewer skilled workers) are needed. Some people have been made unemployed because of this.

I thought I used CAM — but I just had my mac on inside out...

As technology develops, industries will always find ways to take advantage and improve the way they do things. Next up, a bit more on how different industries have changed over the years...

Section 3 — Production and Industry

The Food Industry

With improved transportation and a bit of help from computers, local food in local shops is becoming a thing of the past. I stay well out of it. I grow my own microwave dinners.

The Food Industry has Changed Over Time

1) Before the Industrial Revolution in the 1800s, food products were made on a small scale and sold locally.
2) During the Industrial Revolution farming and manufacturing methods improved — so more food could be produced. The population increased so there was demand for more food products.
3) During the 1800s and 1900s, improvements in transport and food preservation techniques meant it was possible to transport food products to a wider market.
4) It is now usual for food products to be produced on a large scale in one place and then transported for sale over a wide area. Food products are often mass-produced in factories, using new technology like Computer-Aided Manufacture (CAM).

ICT has had a Big Effect on the Food Industry

CAD (Computer-Aided Design) and CAM (Computer-Aided Manufacture) have made it easier to design and make food products.

CAD (Computer-Aided Design)
Computers can help to:
1) design the appearance of a product.
2) compare designs cheaply.
3) calculate nutritional values.
4) calculate the cost of different ideas.
5) produce packaging ideas.
6) send designs via e-mail to production teams around the world.

CAM (Computer-Aided Manufacture)
1) Computers are used to control manufacturing processes, e.g. by using temperature sensors or computerised scales.
2) It's very fast and needs fewer workers — so production costs are lowered.
3) The quality of the product is a set standard.
4) It's hygienic because the food isn't handled.

Manufacturing on a Large Scale Needs a Team of People

There are lots of different jobs in any manufacturing industry (see page 22), but there are a couple more specialists that you need on your team in the food industry to make sure you're making a good product.

- Food Technologists keep the quality of the product high by choosing the methods of production, packaging, storage and distribution.
- Home Economists produce nutritional information for packaging. They also try out new product ideas in a test kitchen.

Takeaway for computers — CAD n' chips...
The food industry (mmmm... industry) has changed a lot, and will probably keep on changing. Especially when I invent a drone that can fly pizzas from the oven straight into my mouth (mmmm... drones).

Manufacturing and Industry

Changes in the textile and materials industries have not only affected the amount and the type of products manufactured, but the ways in which people work and the sort of jobs they do. Zany.

Manufacturing has Changed over Time

1) Since the Industrial Revolution in the 1800s there have been many changes in the manufacturing industry.
2) The manufacture of textiles has moved away from the traditional industrial regions due to improvements in transport and communications.
3) A lot of manufacturing production has moved abroad where labour is cheaper.
4) Improvements in technology have brought several changes.

   - Weaving looms are a lot faster and safer.
   - The use of computers has increased the speed of production (see below).
   - New fabrics and materials have been created, e.g. plastics can now be easily and cheaply made and moulded into any shape.

5) Most products are now produced in high volumes by large companies.

Plastics can be moulded into almost any shape, but obviously the best shape is a dinosaur.

ICT has Influenced the Manufacturing Industry

Computers have speeded up the manufacturing process, from initial design brief to final design.
1) The production of pattern pieces can be done by computers.
2) Computerised cutting tables mean less fabric or material is wasted.
3) Computerised machines mean that highly skilled workers are not always needed.
4) Computers can calculate how much fabric or material has been used and reorder what is needed. This means that the production line keeps going without interruption.

Some Products are Made Using an Assembly Line

1) Assembly lines work by breaking down the complex assembly of a product into lots of small easy steps.
2) Because each task is relatively small and easy, you don't need to employ skilled workers in order to make a product. It also speeds up production.
3) Nowadays, a lot of products are made using assembly lines where each task is done by a computer controlled machine.

Example 1 — Furniture
1) Furniture used to be handmade from beginning to end by highly skilled carpenters.
2) Now, most furniture is manufactured using an assembly line and often sold to consumers unassembled as 'flat-pack' furniture.

Example 2 — Car Manufacture
1) The first car assembly lines appeared in the 1800s.
2) Initially a lot of workers were needed to work the machines.
3) Nowadays, computers control most of the assembly, with reduced numbers of workers.

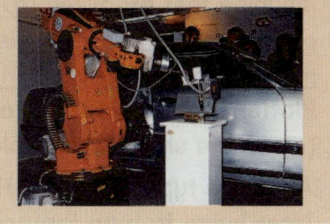

ICT — what Inuits drink on their breaks...

Technology has changed almost every part of the modern world. The changes for industry have been huge. Products can be made better, faster and cheaper. Not this book though. This book was lovingly handcrafted by monks using the finest materials on an island off the coast of Costa Rica. (*That last bit might be a lie*).

Section 3 — Production and Industry

CNC Machines

Right, well you've heard about computers controlling machines over the last few pages. But you can't just plug a laptop into a toaster and tell it to get on with making toast. You need special kinds of machines.

CNC means Computer Numerically Controlled

1) The machines used in the CAM process are Computer Numerically Controlled (CNC).
2) This means the CAD/CAM program works out the necessary movements of the tool head of the machine and sends the data to the machine in the form of numbers.
3) The machine's on-board processor interprets the numbers and controls the movement of the tool head.
4) CNC machines include lathes, milling machines, drilling machines and laser cutters.

There are Different Types of CNC Machine

1) **CNC Lathe** Lathes hold and rotate a material against a tool which shapes the material. They are useful for producing long, cylindrical objects, e.g. table legs.

2) **CNC Miller** Millers hold material on a table that controls the movement of the material against a tool. The material can be moved in three directions past the tool to produce 3D shapes.

A milling machine (the Roland CAMM-3 from TechSoft)

3) **CNC Router** Unlike the lathe and the miller, on a router the material stays still and the tool moves. The rotating tool head moves in three directions to cut the material and produce 3D shapes, e.g. a router can be used to produce a wooden printing block for stamping patterns on textiles.

A router/miller (the Roland Modela PRO from TechSoft)

4) **3D Printer** Like a CNC miller, a 3D printer produces 3D shapes. Unlike the miller, the 3D printer makes the object by adding layers of materials on top of one another.

5) **CNC Knitting Machine** A computer-controlled knitting machine or weaving loom can be used to manufacture patterned fabric.

6) **CNC Plotter/Cutter** A plotter/cutter is a CNC machine that produces 2D objects from thin sheets of plastic, card or fabric. The machine cutter moves left and right and the material moves forward and back to cut out the 2D object. Plotter/cutters are used to produce patterns, stencils and nets (a net is a shape which folds up to make a 3D object, e.g. a box)

A special type of CNC cutter is a laser cutter, which uses a laser beam to burn through a sheet of material to create a 2D object.

A CNC plotter/cutter

I'm lathing — not boring...

The link between CAD and CAM means you can change parts of the design program and specialised software will automatically update the CNC machine. Wish I'd invented that, I'd be filthy rich.

Section 3 — Production and Industry

Health and Safety

Manufacturers and businesses have a responsibility to look after the health and safety of their employees and customers. It might not be a barrel of laughs but it's really important to get right.

Think About Safety When You Make a Product

Salad preparation can be dangerous.

1) Health and safety are important parts of planning a product. Checks should be carried out as part of the production process, e.g. that equipment is working properly and machinery is in good condition.

2) Hazard Analysis Critical Control Points (HACCP) is a system that manufacturers use to spot possible dangers in the manufacturing process before they happen. They can then take action to reduce the risk of something going wrong.

Carry Out a Risk Assessment

1) Find out which processes might be hazardous before you start making your product.
2) Evaluate the risks involved in the production process.
3) Take precautions. This minimises the chance of an accident happening.
4) This process is called carrying out a risk assessment.
5) Risk assessments have to be carried out in industry to make sure the manufacturing process is as safe as possible for employees.

Basic Health and Safety Precautions

1) Wear goggles when using machinery and dust masks and gloves as appropriate.
2) For food preparation, wear an apron to hold loose clothing down and tie long hair back.
3) Secure work being drilled using a hand vice, machine vice or G-clamp.
4) Don't lift more weight than you can manage or put a lot of strain on your back.
5) Know how to switch off and isolate machines in an emergency.
6) Store away materials and equipment safely. Dispose of waste properly.

Follow Simple Rules to Keep Food Safe

1) Some basic do's and don'ts — wear a clean apron, tie hair back and cover it, wash your hands before handling food, never lick your fingers, cover cuts with waterproof dressings, don't cough or smoke around food, and don't work with food if you are ill.
2) Never use food after its use-by date.
3) Avoid cross-contamination between raw and cooked foods by using separate tools, equipment and surfaces for each. Wash your hands after touching raw meat.
4) Make sure equipment and tools are properly cleaned to prevent any contamination.
5) Carefully control the temperature food is kept at. Try to stop bacteria multiplying by keeping food out of the danger zone of 5 to 63 °C.
6) Pack and transport raw and cooked food separately — using a cool box (manufacturers would use a refrigerated lorry).

Cross-contamination is when bacteria are passed from one food to another.

Sounds like licking the blender's not allowed then...

Get this health and safety stuff learnt and learnt well, it's important. If your product keeps me on the bog for a week while I vomit in the sink I'm not going to even look at your brand again — OK.

Section 3 — Production and Industry

Environmental Concerns

Most types of industry have an impact on the environment.

Industry has a Big Effect on the Environment

1) Natural fuel resources like coal, oil and gas (fossil fuels) are needed for power to process raw materials and to produce packaging — but they are running out and create pollution when used to produce energy.
2) Factories use energy and create their own pollution e.g. noise, dust, fumes etc.
3) Products are now transported all over the world. The planes, lorries and ships used burn fossil fuels and pollute the environment — the further a product is transported, the more pollution it causes.
4) The processes of spinning, weaving and knitting use chemicals to lubricate the machinery and to protect the fibres during production. Chemicals are also used to finish different materials, e.g. varnish. These chemicals need to be used and disposed of in a safe manner to avoid polluting the environment.
5) Dyeing fabric uses large amounts of water. The waste water contains chemicals and dye which can pollute the environment if it's not controlled.
6) Getting the raw materials to make your product in the first place can also harm the environment, e.g.

- Farmers spray pesticides and herbicides on fields to kill pests and weeds. This can seriously harm wildlife.
- Plastics are made from oil. When the oil is extracted, an accident can cause oil spills which can damage sea life. Producing plastics can also produce a lot of chemical waste.
- Wood is obtained from chopping down trees, which can destroy wildlife habitats and contribute to climate change.

Consumers Worry about GM Foods

1) Some plants are genetically modified (GM). This means scientists have changed or replaced some of the genes which control what the plant is like. Plants can be designed to have useful properties such as resistance to insects, viruses and disease.
2) Some consumers and environmentalists are concerned about GM foods. Pollen from the GM plants contains the modified genes. This pollen could fertilise normal plants. This could result in the creation of 'superweeds'.
3) Biodiversity is the variety of animals and plants living in a habitat. Some folk are concerned that if farmers focus on mass-producing GM crops, then some species of plant and animal may die out. This would damage the biodiversity.

I'm walking proof that GM foods are harmless.

Packaging can be a lot more Environmentally Friendly

1) 70% of British household rubbish is waste packaging. Packaging made of plastic is often thrown away after one use, and takes years to biodegrade.
2) Packaging doesn't have to be so bad for the environment. Here's some ways designers can help:

   1) Use recycled materials — so you're not using up new resources.
   2) Use recyclable materials — so that the consumer can recycle them.
   3) Use biodegradable materials which decay quickly after being thrown away.
   4) Use refillable containers, e.g. plastic washing-liquid bottles that can be refilled from recyclable cardboard cartons.
   5) Use only the minimum packaging necessary.
   6) Include a note on the packaging reminding the consumer to reuse or recycle it after use.

Hmmm, it's not the cheeriest page is it...

... but it is important. Fear not — next up is what we can do to avoid damaging the environment...

Section 3 — Production and Industry

Environmental Concerns

Manufacturers can Help the Environment

1) Manufacturers can carry out a life-cycle analysis to find out what effect a product has on the environment. It includes all stages of the product's life — design, raw materials, manufacture, packaging, storage, transport, sale, use and disposal.
2) The life-cycle analysis can be used to work out ways to make the product more environmentally friendly, e.g.

- They could reduce the amount of water, chemicals and energy used.
- Natural substances such as enzymes could be used instead of chemicals in finishing processes (see page 35).
- They could use biodegradable chemicals.
- They could try to remove chemicals such as dyes from waste water more effectively.
- Products which have been produced in an environmentally friendly way could be labelled as such.
- Using wood from sustainable forests (a forest where a tree is planted for every one cut down).

Remember the 6 Rs

The '6 R's help manufacturers think about how to reduce a product's impact on the environment:

Reduce — is there a way of reducing the amount of material the product uses?
Rethink — is there an alternative to this product that is less damaging to the environment?
Refuse — this means refusing to use methods or materials that are bad for the environment.
Recycle — could the product be made from recycled materials, or recycled once it's been used?
Reuse — could the product be reprocessed to make something else?
Repair — is the product easy to repair?

Consumers can Help the Environment too

It's not just manufacturers who can help make the world a better place. Here are just a few of the ways consumers can help too...

Food
1) Buying only the food you need, so there is less waste.
2) Buying local food to keep transport down.
3) Recycle food waste e.g. keep a compost heap.

Materials
1) Reusing plastic carrier bags when shopping, or not using them at all.
2) Buying food with less packaging or recyclable packaging — this helps keep waste levels down.

Textiles
1) Materials can be recycled to make new textile products.
2) Old textiles can be given a new lease of life with new decoration.
3) Synthetic fibres can sometimes be regenerated into new fabric.
4) Cellulose and protein fibres (like cotton) are biodegradable — they break down into the soil. This means they are environmentally friendly to dispose of because they won't take up space in a waste dump for years.
5) Consumers can also help by buying environmentally friendly products.

OK, maybe it's time to recycle my old corduroy pyjamas...

Environmental issues are pretty darned important. We can't just go about polluting the environment for the sake of fashion. I'd guess it's quite important in terms of your product too. Hint hint.

Section 3 — Production and Industry

Section 4 — Resistant Materials

Classifying Materials

You can classify materials by their properties, their uses and where they come from. There are four main types of material used in resistant materials work — and this is how they're usually classified...

Metals can be Ferrous or Non-Ferrous

1) Metals are obtained from the Earth's crust as metal ore. The metals need to be extracted from the ore.
2) Metals can be mixed together to make new materials with different properties, called alloys.
3) Ferrous metals contain iron which make them magnetic.
   Non-Ferrous metals don't contain iron and are not magnetic.

Metal	Alloy/Pure Metal	Ferrous?	Properties	Uses
Mild Steel	carbon + iron	Yes	strong, cheap, rusts	bridges, car bodies, trains
Copper	pure metal	No	good conductor, easily bent, doesn't rust	pipes, electrical wiring
Aluminium	pure metal	No	lightweight, doesn't rust, strong, expensive	aeroplanes, ladders, drinks cans
Brass	copper + zinc	No	strong, doesn't rust	door handles, electrical parts
Stainless Steel	iron + carbon + chromium	Yes	hard, doesn't rust	pans, cutlery, fixtures for boats

Wood — There are Two Types, Softwood and Hardwood

SOFTWOOD → From evergreen trees, like pine (fast-growing) → Used for furniture, garden sheds, floorboards

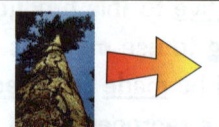

HARDWOOD → From deciduous trees, like oak, ash and beech (slow-growing) → Used for more expensive furniture, tool handles and toys

Plastics are Man-Made Using Crude Oil

1) Thermoplastics can be formed into shapes when hot and can be reformed by reheating, e.g.
   - polythene (polyethylene) — used for bags, bottles, bowls
   - PVC (polyvinyl chloride) — used for pipes and gutters
   - polystyrene — used for foam packaging, outer cases of radios

2) Thermosetting plastics can be formed into shape, but once they've set they can't be changed, e.g.
   - polyester resin — used in car bodies, boats
   - urea formaldehyde — used in electrical sockets

Composites are Made by Combining Materials

1) Composites are different materials combined to create a new material with different properties.
2) The different materials in a composite are sometimes glued together.
   E.g. internal doors are a combination of plywood faces, a wooden frame and a paper honeycomb centre, all glued together. The result is a lightweight, strong, shock-resistant, wood-look material.

Cos we are living in a material world...

This might not be the most scintillating of pages but it's important to know your materials, so get learning.

Selecting Materials

Wood is great for shelves, but it'd make a lousy saucepan. You've got to think about what properties your product needs, and then find a material that has those properties. Wooden barbecue? NO.

Materials are Chosen for Their Properties

1) Materials are chosen because they have the right properties for a product, e.g. the material used for a bridge needs to be strong and durable.
2) Think about what the product you are making has to do, the type of environment it will be used in and how long it is expected to last. Write a list of the properties your product should have.
3) Once you've worked out what properties your product needs, you can select a material that has those properties to make it from.

> **Real-life examples**
> 1) The Forth Bridge is made of steel. Steel was used because it's strong, cheap, easily joined and weathers well if protected (in this case with paint — see p.35).
> 2) Lego® bricks are made of plastic. Plastic is used because it's durable, cheap, easily formed into complex shapes, non toxic and colourful.
> 3) Garden sheds are often made of softwood. This material is used because it's cheap, easy to put together and can be coated to protect it from bad weather.

Think About the Cost, Function and Look of Your Product

Property / Characteristic	Questions to keep you awake at night
Strength	Does your product have to withstand forces, e.g. twisting and pulling?
Weight	Does your product have to be light enough to carry around?
Durability	Will your product have to withstand a lot of wear and tear?
Flexibility	Should your product be able to fold up, or bend?
Aesthetics	Should your product be a particular colour, texture or style?
Cost	Does the product need to be cheap?
Availability	Is the material you want available locally?
Health and Safety impact	Will the material you're thinking about make a safe product?
Environmental impact	Is the material you want to use environmentally-friendly? E.g. biodegradable

You Often Have to Compromise when Selecting Materials

1) Selecting a material can be tricky if there are lots of different properties you would like the material to have — it's often hard to find a material which has all of them.
2) You often have to compromise when selecting a material, e.g. choosing a less attractive material because it's cheaper.

Compromise — an action movie featuring cute puppies...
Life is all about compromise, unfortunately. You might want to make your phone case out of glow-in-the-dark, heat-sensitive, rainbow-coloured plastic, but you'll probably have to settle for boring old PVC.

Section 4 — Resistant Materials

Modern Materials

Those crazy scientist-types keep developing whole ranges of new materials, with oodles of new properties. We can now design products that weren't even thinkable with traditional materials.

Smart Materials are Developed to Have Useful Properties

Smart materials have been developed which change their properties in response to changes in their environment. Now is that cool or what — bring on the self-cleaning crockery.

1) Shape memory alloy is a smart material that is able to "remember" its original shape. It can be easily bent when cool, but when heated returns to its original shape — if only my hair could do that. E.g. Smart wire changes shape when electricity passes through it. It's used in robot hands to make the fingers grip objects.

2) Silicon is a semi-conductor — meaning its resistance to electric current decreases as the temperature increases. Silicon crystals are used to make tiny electric circuit boards (silicon chips).

I just don't know how we used to get by before robot hands

Fibreglass and Carbon Fibre are Composite Materials

1) Fibreglass (glass-reinforced polyester) is made from thin glass fibres stuck together with a polyester resin. It's a very strong material that can be formed into complex shapes, e.g. boat hulls, swimming pool water chutes and slides

2) Using carbon fibres instead of glass fibres produces an even stronger material which is very lightweight. Carbon fibre is used for racing car bodies, helmets and bulletproof vests.

Loads of Research and Development Goes into this Stuff

1) Modern materials with new properties are great for designers. It means they can design products which weren't possible before, e.g. they can make tennis rackets that are really lightweight (unlike the old wooden ones).

2) Research and development of new materials is often aimed at creating materials with particular properties. This is because research is often sponsored by companies and manufacturers. They want materials to be developed which will be useful for their sorts of products.

Modern materials — they're soooooo next year...

Imagine being a Formula 1® driver when they started making racing cars out of reinforced plastics. One minute you're struggling to get your metal beast round those corners... next you're zooming round sharp bends in your mega-light machine, generating 5g sideways forces, and wishing you'd had a smaller breakfast.

Section 4 — Resistant Materials

Changing Properties

You can change the properties of a material by heating, cooling, moulding and reinforcing it or combining it with another material. Mmmmm. Marmite®. Combined with crumpets.

Thermoforming Processes Use Heat to Shape Materials

When you heat thermoplastics, they become soft and pliable. You can make loads of shapes out of plastic using thermoforming processes ('thermoforming' means changing the shape using heat).

1) **INJECTION MOULDING** Hot, soft plastic is squirted into a mould. When the plastic cools it sets and can be taken out of the mould.

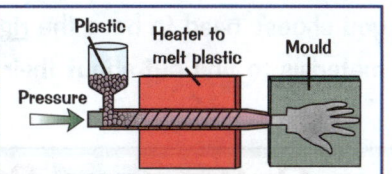

See page 37 for more on injection moulding.

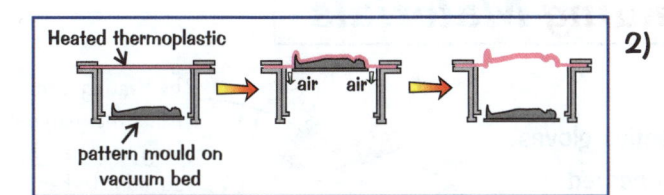

2) **VACUUM FORMING** A vacuum forming machine heats a plastic sheet until it's soft and then creates a vacuum underneath it (this means the air pressure is removed). Air pressure on top of the plastic then pushes it down over the mould.

3) **BLOW MOULDING** A sheet of plastic is heated until soft and placed under a mould. Air is blown under it, forcing the plastic up into the mould. This process is used to make bottles and containers.

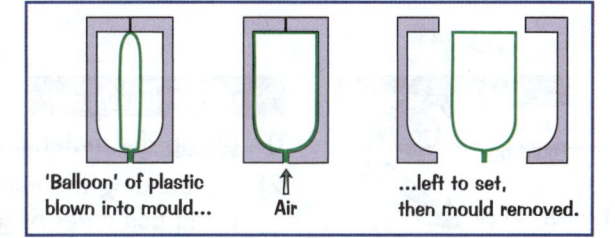

The Properties of Metals Can be Changed with Heat

Metals can be heat-treated to change their properties, e.g.
- Hardening — metal is heated and then rapidly cooled in cold water to harden it.
- Annealing — metal is softened by heating it and leaving it to cool gradually.
- Tempering — metal is heated to make it tougher and less likely to break. Tempering is often used for steel.

Combining Materials Creates New Properties

1) Materials can be combined by sandwiching them in layers to create a new material.

2) Gluing thin sheets of aluminium on each side of a paper honeycomb creates a new material that is very strong and lightweight. It was designed for train floors and aeroplane parts.

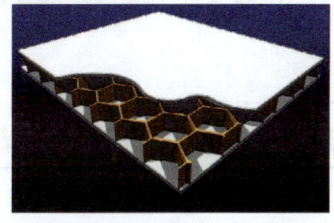

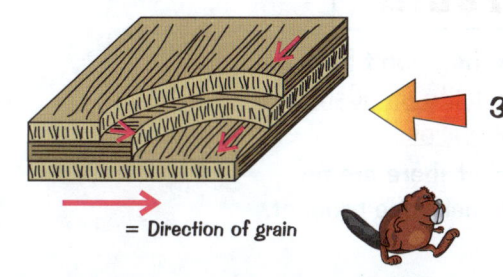

3) Plywood is made of layers of wood stuck together. Although it's thin, it's very strong because layers are arranged with the grain going in alternate directions. To make plywood even stronger, a layer of fibre glass can be added.

= Direction of grain

Changing Properties — This week Kirstie Allsopp is heat-treated...
Combining materials is a really useful trick for improving properties, e.g. you can reinforce concrete with steel bars to make it stronger. [Note to artist — no more vacuum forming people.]

Section 4 — Resistant Materials

Testing the Properties of Materials

Different materials have different properties. These are sometimes called working characteristics, but not by me so I won't bang on about it. Test away to find materials with the right properties for you.

Test Materials to Find Out their Properties

1) The design specification (page 10) for a product gives details of the properties the product should have.
2) The materials you choose need to have the right properties for your product.
3) Test different materials to find out about their properties.

Try Heating, Cutting and Bending Materials

Test the effect of heating

1) Hold the material over a line bender, using protective gloves.
2) Some materials will soften and bend easily when heated.

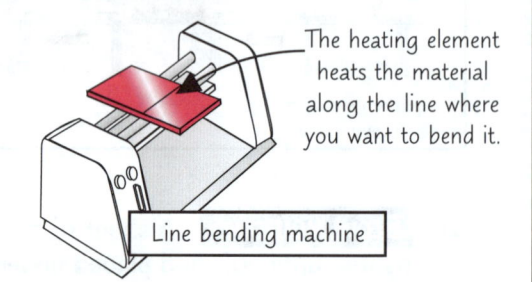

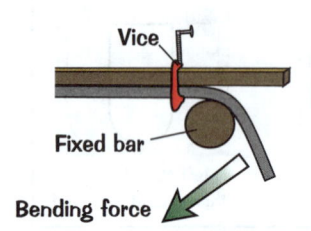

The heating element heats the material along the line where you want to bend it.

Line bending machine

Test for flexibility

1) Clamp the material in a vice on a workbench.
2) Try bending the material by hand, or you could use a set of weights, or even a hammer.

Test for hardness

1) Place the material in a vice and use a file or saw to try cutting or wearing down the material.
2) How easy or difficult it is to cut will tell you how hard the material is.

Filing

Make sure it's a fair test

1) Variables must be the same each time, with only one difference — e.g. the material being tested. Variables are things that might affect the results of the test, e.g. temperature, size of material.
2) Record your results accurately in a table.
3) Carry out the test a number of times for each material. Take out any results which look like freak results and find the average of the rest.

In Industry Materials are Tested for Faults

1) In industry, materials and components are tested to make sure they don't have any faults, e.g. cracks or rust. This ensures that the final product meets quality standards. It's especially important for materials used in car and aeroplane engines.
2) Tests are sometimes done using X-ray machines. They check that there are no tiny fractures or imperfections in the materials or parts used to make the product.

TEST IT — a tiny gap could mean the end of the worl d...
Take a tip from industry and check your materials don't have any flaws before you make your product. No massive holes through the middle. Or mysterious orange patches. Or alien inhabitants.

Section 4 — Resistant Materials

Finishing Techniques & the Environment

Most products need to look good, and be protected from damage (to stop them rusting and suchlike). Putting on a finish can sort that out, but it can also pollute the environment — swings and roundabouts.

Finishes Give Materials Protection and Good Looks

1) The finish is an extra layer, coating or decoration added to the outside of a material to protect it and make it look good. The finish improves the properties of the material.
2) The type of finish used depends on the type of material and the purpose of the product.
3) Most finishes are added with a brush, cloth or spray. The main exceptions are dip-coating where hot metal is dipped into powdered plastic, and electroplating where a metal coating is deposited on the surface of another metal using an electric current.

MATERIAL	POSSIBLE FINISHES	PROPERTIES OF FINISH	ENVIRONMENTAL IMPACT
Metals	paint	waterproof, adds colour, protects from rust	pollutant when liquid
	plastic coating/ dip coating	hard-wearing, waterproof	plastic not biodegradable
	laquer (similar to varnish)	waterproof	pollutant when liquid
	electroplating	more resistant to rust, looks like different metal	chemicals used are toxic
Wood	paint	waterproof, adds colour	pollutant when liquid
	varnish	waterproof, makes wood more attractive	pollutant when liquid
	oil	fairly waterproof, makes grain show up	little or no pollution
	wax	gives polished finish	little or no pollution

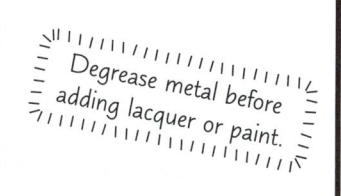

Degrease metal before adding lacquer or paint.

Thoroughly sand down wood before applying a finish.

Manufacturing Has an Impact on the Environment

1) The manufacturing, using and disposing of products can have a negative effect on the environment.
2) The more processes a material goes through, the more fossil fuels will be burnt in its manufacture. That means more polluting gases (e.g. carbon monoxide) are released into the environment. For example, an electroplated metal table needs more energy to make than a hand-built wooden one.
3) The production of plastics creates chemical waste, and the plastics aren't biodegradable — that means anything you coat in plastic will stay in the environment or landfill sites for yonks.
4) Paint, lacquer, varnish and other liquids are chemicals — they're pollutants when they're liquid, which means they can harm the environment if they get into sewage or rivers.

Designers and Consumers Can Help the Environment

1) Designers can create products that need less energy to make and use.
2) Products can be made with recycled, or recyclable, materials.
3) Consumers can buy environmentally-friendly products, and remember to recycle materials.
4) There's more on this on pages 28-29.

I see a red door and I want to paint it black...

...but I'd get nasty paint fumes everywhere. Then I'd clean my brush in white spirit and I might accidentally spill some on the garden and kill all the plants and... (sigh) maybe I'll just leave it red...

Section 4 — Resistant Materials

Joining

Before making complex products, you need to know how to join and combine materials. When you know your mortise and tenon from a dovetail joint — then you'll be ready.

You Can Join Wood with Joints

There are lots of different types of joints. Marking out and cutting them takes a lot skill. Accuracy is vital to make them fit well and look good.

1) Butt joints are simple but not very strong. Used for cheap tables.

2) Mitre joints are used for picture frames.

3) Lap joints are used for boxes and drawers.

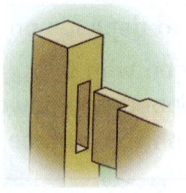

4) Mortise and Tenon joints are very strong and used for tables and chairs.

5) Dovetail joints are strong and look attractive. Often used for drawers.

Joints are often glued or nailed together to make them more permanent. There are lots of ways to do this:

Different Types of Glue

1) PVA (polyvinyl acetate) is a wood glue that can also be used for card.
2) Cascamite is a synthetic (man-made) resin that's stronger than PVA, and waterproof.
3) Tensol cement is a special glue for acrylic.

Screws, Nails, Nuts and Bolts

1) Nuts and bolts provide temporary fixings for metal.
2) Nails are usually made from mild steel and are used for wood. They have a straight shank (shaft).
3) Screws produce a stronger join than nails. The shank has a thread (spiral groove) around the outside.
4) Countersunk screws give a flush (flat) surface finish. The head of the screw lies slightly below the surface of the wood.

a screw — head, shank (shaft), thread

Rivets, Soldering and Welding are for Joining Metal

RIVETS Rivets are metal pegs with a head on one end. They are used for permanently fixing metal pieces together. A hole is drilled through both pieces of metal and the rivet is inserted. The head is held against the metal while the other end is flattened and shaped into another head on the other side of the join.

SOLDERING Solder (made from tin and lead) is melted onto the components to be joined, sticking them together when it cools and solidifies. A soldering iron or blow torch can be used for this process.

WELDING Welding uses very high temperatures to melt the edges of the joint so that they flow together. Thinned metal, or any small gaps, are filled with molten metal from a welding rod. This is the strongest method of joining metal.

Butt joints — joined at the hip...

Joining stuff together — sounds simple, but there are lots of ways to do it and it needs to be done right. After all, I wouldn't fancy sitting on a poorly put together chair, never mind fly on a poorly put together plane.

Section 4 — Resistant Materials

Forming

Forming means changing the shape of a material. You can use heat, pressure and shaping techniques to do this. Or — if you eat your crusts like granny told you — your bare hands.

Deforming and Reforming are Different

1) Forming — this simply means shaping a material.
2) Deforming — changing the shape of a material without any loss of material, e.g. vacuum forming plastic or bending a sheet of metal.
3) Reforming — this involves changing the state of a material, e.g. from a liquid to a solid, as in casting (see below).

Casting is a Method of Shaping Metal or Plastic

Casting produces shapes by pouring molten metal or thermoplastic into a mould and allowing it to cool. When the material cools, it sets into the shape of the mould.

> E.g. Sand casting
> - A pattern is made and packed in moulding sand.
> - The pattern is removed, leaving a shape in the moulding sand, which can be filled with molten metal. The metal cools and hardens into the shape left by the pattern.
> - The most common metals used for casting in schools are aluminium and pewter.

Injection Moulding is a Method of Shaping Plastic

1) Injection moulding involves injecting molten thermoplastic into a metal mould under pressure. The plastic is often melted using built-in heaters. When the plastic cools it sets into the shape of the mould.
2) Injection moulding is used in industry to mass produce items like telephones, vacuum cleaners, buckets and phone casings.
3) Thermoplastics like polythene, polystyrene, polypropylene, and nylon are used.

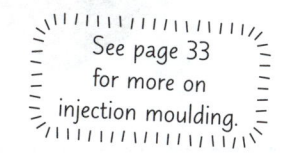

See page 33 for more on injection moulding.

Press Moulding is Used to Shape Thermosetting Plastic

1) Thermosetting plastic powder is put into a mould.
2) A former is pressed onto it and pushes the plastic into the mould.
3) Very high temperatures and pressures liquify the powder, and the plastic is set into a permanent shape.

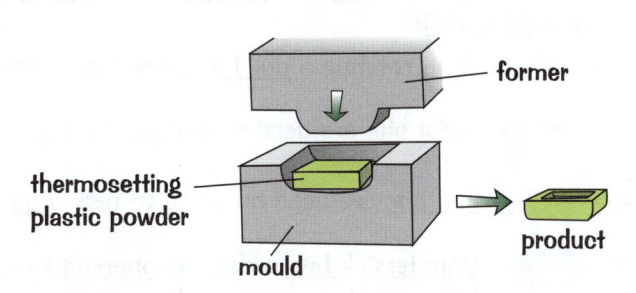

Cats' throats — great at Purr-forming...

Once you've designed and made your mould, you can produce batches of identical products like keyrings. Or £2 coins... but, y'know, that's a lot more difficult and a lot more illegal than the keyring option.

Section 4 — Resistant Materials

Tools and Equipment

There is a huge range of tools and equipment out there to cut, shape and form materials.

Materials Can be Cut Using Hand Tools...

Saws are the main cutting tools. There are different saws for different materials:

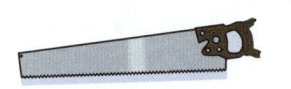

Saws have to be kept sharp, either by sharpening or replacing the blade.

Panel saw — for wood

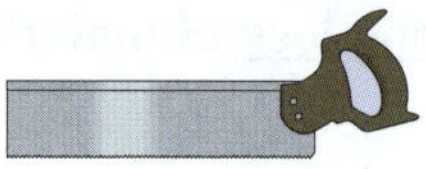

Tenon saw — for wood

Hacksaw — for metals and plastics

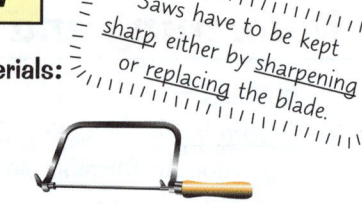

Coping saw — for cutting curves in wood or plastic

Rough edges from sawing can be tidied up by sanding.

...and Machine Tools

1) Circular saws and saw benches have round blades and are used to cut wood and boards like plywood. They make straight cuts only.
2) Band saws have blades in long flexible loops. They come in different widths and can make straight or curved cuts.
3) A jig saw has changeable blades and different speeds. You can make straight or curved cuts in all materials, but it's quite slow.

Circular saw

Jig saw

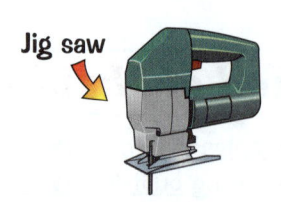

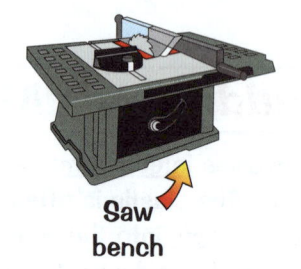

Saw bench

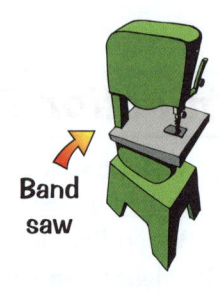

Band saw

Drills Make Holes (no kidding)

1) To help you drill in the right place, you can make a pilot hole first using a bradawl (for wood or plastic) or a centre punch (for metal). 
2) Depending on how hard the material is, you can do the actual drilling with a brace, a hand drill or a power drill (e.g. a pillar drill).
3) All drills work by rotating a drill bit against the material.

Brace

Hand drill

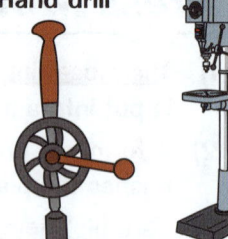

Pillar drill

Twist bits are used to drill small holes in wood, metal or plastic.

Flat bits are used on wood to drill large flat-bottomed holes.

Countersink bits widen the opening to an existing hole, allowing screw heads to sit flat on the surface.

I came, I sawed, I countersinked...

There are different tools for doing different things, or working with different materials — it's a no-brainer. You wouldn't try to eat soup with a fork, or steak with a whisk, would you? I am tempted to try though...

Section 4 — Resistant Materials

Tools and Equipment

It's all plane-sailing from here on out (get it?). A couple more handy tools and machines to learn about before the end of another section. There are plenty pretty pictures to help you out here — no excuses.

Materials Can be Shaped Using Hand Tools

1) Wood chisels come in different shapes for making different cuts. You hit them with a mallet (a type of hammer with a large head, usually made from wood or rubber).

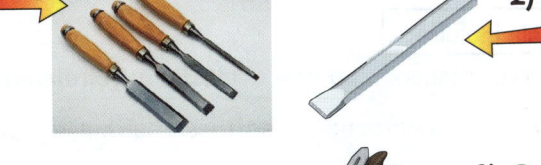

2) Cold chisels are used on metals — they're hit with a hammer.

3) Gougers are chisels with a curved cutting edge — they're used for sculpting.

4) Bench planes have angled blades that shave off thin layers of material. They're used to shape wood.

5) Files have hundreds of small teeth to cut away at a material. Different 'cuts' of file are used for different processes — rough cuts are for removing material and fine cuts are for final smoothing. Files are usually used on metals, plastics and wood and they come in all sorts of shapes and sizes.

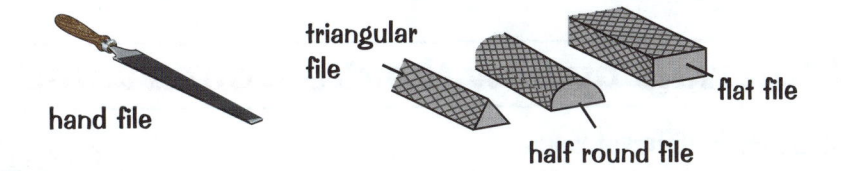

hand file

triangular file

half round file

flat file

Materials Can Also be Shaped Using Machine Tools

A planer and thicknesser (either separate or both in a single machine) are used to remove material from the surface of pieces of wood to give a consistent cross section.

A milling machine is used to remove one thin layer of material at a time to produce the required size or shape. It can also be used to make a surface absolutely flat. Milling machines produce a very accurate finish.

A bench grinder contains abrasive wheels of different grades (coarse to smooth). It's used to remove metal for shaping or finishing purposes, as well as for sharpening edged tools such as chisels.

Lathes are used to cut and shape materials to produce rounded objects, e.g. chair legs. The material is held and rotated by the lathe and the turning tool or cutting bit is pressed onto the material.

You need to be well drilled in this stuff...

There's nothing here to blow your mind — saws cut stuff up and drills make holes. Pretty simple really. Make sure you don't skimp when you're learning the details though — it's all important stuff.

Section 4 — Resistant Materials

Section 5 — Textiles

Classifying Materials

Materials can be classified into different groups so they're easier to compare. They're classified by stuff like their properties, their uses, their construction and their source — but rarely by newt resistance.

Classify Materials by their Properties

The properties of materials are the way they behave, look and feel.

Properties of materials include:

appearance   crease resistance   texture   elasticity (stretchiness)   flammability
strength   durability   absorbency   softness/hardness   washability   warmth

E.g.

Material	Uses	Properties
Cotton	clothes, sheets, tablecloths	durable, absorbent, strong
Wool	jumpers, blankets, hats	warm, absorbent, flammable
Nylon	tents, raincoats, backpacks	strong, durable, washable
LYCRA®	sportswear, socks, belts	elastic, soft, lightweight

Classify Materials by how they're Constructed

Materials are constructed in different ways:
1) Woven fabrics are two sets of yarns (called the warp and the weft) woven under and over each other to create a fabric. Types of weave include plain weave and twill weave.
2) Knitted fabrics are yarns knitted together using needles or a knitting machine.
3) Non-woven fabrics are created by bonding or felting fibres together.

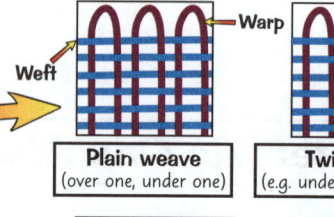

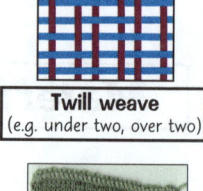

Plain weave (over one, under one)
Twill weave (e.g. under two, over two)
Weaving
Knitting

Classify Materials by their Source

You can classify materials by their source — whether they are natural or man-made.

Natural Fibres
1) Animal — wool from animals, e.g. sheep, alpaca, Angora goats and cashmere goats.
2) Vegetable — fibres from plants, e.g. linen, cotton, hessian.

Man-made Fibres
1) Regenerated — natural fibres that have been industrially processed, e.g. viscose, acetate.
2) Synthetic — fibres completely man-made using chemicals, e.g. nylon, polyester, acrylic, elastane.

Synthetic fibres can have the appearance of natural fibres but with improvements in price or properties:
1) Polyester looks like cotton, but it creases less easily and is cheaper to produce.
2) Nylon looks like silk, but it's generally much stronger and more durable.

Polyester — my crease-proof parrot...

Next time you go shopping, have a look at the labels in clothes. Compare cotton to polyester, guess how clothes were made and talk about their properties. Yes, go shopping. It's schoolwork.

World Materials

This isn't rocket science — <u>where you live</u> affects what you need to wear. Believe it or not thermal underpants weren't invented in a hot country, and bikinis aren't a must-buy in Alaska.

Local Needs, Resources and Culture Affect Textiles

1) Textile products are manufactured in areas with different cultures, needs and resources. So <u>designs</u> and <u>manufacturing processes</u> are different in different places, even for the same type of clothing.

2) Factors affecting <u>local textile production</u> include:

> the environment (e.g. if it's hot, cold or rains a lot)   what's fashionable   local consumer needs
>
> culture and tradition   what fibres are grown/produced locally   what equipment is available

3) You can find good examples of this by looking at the <u>history</u> of <u>textile production</u>. E.g.

<u>Denim clothing</u> was originally made in <u>America</u> to provide <u>hard-wearing</u> work clothes for farm labourers. It is made of <u>cotton</u> — which was cheap and produced locally.

In <u>traditional Indian textiles colour</u> was <u>symbolic</u> — different colours had different meanings, e.g. red was associated with good luck, and saffron (yellow) with spring.

The <u>Inuits</u> made clothes using <u>leather</u> and <u>fur</u>. These materials were <u>available</u> and suited the environment because they were very <u>warm</u>.

Textile Production has Changed Over Time

1) Nowadays, textile products aren't always made for local consumers. Modern <u>communications</u> and <u>transport</u> allow big companies to operate worldwide. They can <u>design</u> a product in one country, <u>manufacture</u> it somewhere else and <u>sell</u> it in many different countries.

2) Advances in <u>technology</u> have affected textile production. Manufacturers now often use <u>man-made fibres</u> to make their products, instead of locally produced natural fibres like wool and cotton.

3) <u>Fashion</u>, and what is <u>socially acceptable</u>, changes over time. This affects textile manufacturing. E.g. Skirt lengths in Britain changed dramatically over the last century — clothes are made now that would have been socially <u>unacceptable</u> back in the day.

1910s   1950s   1960s   now

A mankini isn't socially acceptable anywhere...

Take a butcher's at what you're wearing and see if you can find labels saying <u>where</u> it was made — I bet you 10p it won't be the UK... WAIT, no put them back on. Strewth your feet reek.

Section 5 — Textiles

Selecting Materials

Before choosing which fabric to use, you need to find out whether it has the right properties for the job. You don't want to spend forever making a beautiful cotton umbrella, then find that cotton leaks.

Think about these Criteria when Selecting Materials

The main things to think about when choosing a material are:

FUNCTION — The fabric needs to have properties which suit the use of the product, e.g. waterproof, crease resistant, hard-wearing or flame-resistant.

AESTHETICS — It needs to look and feel good. This is more important for some products than others, e.g. fashionable clothes need to look good, work overalls don't.

COST — It needs to be affordable. The selling price and expected sales of the final product will decide how expensive the materials used can be.

AVAILABILITY — It needs to be easily available in sufficient quantities.

MANUFACTURE — The equipment to process the fabric needs to be available, and you need to have the skills to use it.

> In reality you often won't find a material with all the properties you want. You'll have to compromise, e.g. choose a material that doesn't have all the aesthetic properties you want but is available and affordable.

Think About Properties when Selecting Materials

Fibres in fabrics have different properties, making them better for some uses than others. The fabrics used in the products below all have properties suitable for their use.

DENSITY — The weight of the material. Dense fabric is bulky and heavy.

ABSORBENCY — How well a fibre can soak up moisture.

COLOUR — Most natural fibres are off-white, cream or brownish. Manufactured fibres are almost colourless but dye pigments can be added.

FLAMMABILITY — How easily a fibre will burn.

ELASTICITY — The amount a fibre can be stretched and still return to its original length.

TENACITY — The amount of force needed to break a fibre. High tenacity means good durability.

RESILIENCE — How well fibres return to their original shape after being bent. This is also called crease resistance.

Choose life, choose a job, choose a material...

To really understand about properties, empty your wardrobe. Don't put any of the stuff back until you know exactly why each material was chosen. You could even make a little checklist, if you like.

Section 5 — Textiles

Testing Properties

Test fabrics to find out about their properties. Now I'll say that again, only bigger...

Test Fabrics to find out about their Properties

1) The design specification for a product gives details of the properties the product should have.
2) The fabric you make your product out of needs to have the right properties.
3) You can test different materials to find out about their properties.
   This will help you decide which material best fits the design specification.

Make Sure it's a Fair Test

1) Variables must be the same each time, with only one difference — the material being tested.
   (Variables are things that might affect the results of the test, e.g. temperature, size of fabric.)
2) Record your results accurately and write them down in a table.
3) Carry out the test a number of times for each fabric.
   That way if you get any crazy results, you'll realise they're wrong.

Tests to Find Out About Specific Properties

1) WATER RESISTANCE

Stretch your fabric over the top of a jam jar and drip 5 cm^3 of water on it. Measure how much water passes into the jar in one minute. Water resistance is an important property for coats, umbrellas, tents and backpacks.

2) CREASE RESISTANCE

Scrunch up your fabric and see how easily it springs back. Crease resistance is important for products that need to look smart.

3) ABRASION RESISTANCE AND DURABILITY

Stretch your fabric over a wooden block and rub it with a pumice stone for 30 seconds. Record the effect — whether the fabric is bobbled, torn or retaining its original appearance. Durability is useful for clothes that have to withstand a lot of wear and tear, e.g. gardening clothes.

4) WASHABILITY AND COLOUR-FASTNESS

Wash samples of your fabric in different temperatures of water. See if they shrink, stretch, crease or lose their colour. Washability is an important property for things that get wet (like swimwear) and everyday clothes.

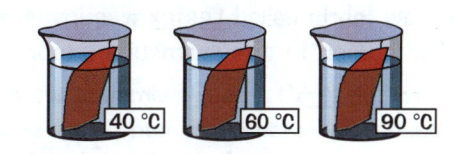

Property — not that fake brown stuff...

You can test for loads of other things too — elasticity, flammability, reaction to sunlight, immortality. I saw an immortal tool once, it looked miserable and glittered when directly exposed to sunlight.

Section 5 — Textiles

Modern Materials

Back in the old days people used to wear vests made from grass and mammoth's armpit hair — itchy, but it's all different nowadays. Yep, now we have "modern materials", not a mammoth hair in sight.

New Materials have been Created with New Properties

1) New textiles have been developed with modern technology.
2) Modern textiles are designed to have useful properties and characteristics. E.g. TENCEL® is a relatively environmentally-friendly modern fabric which has the following combination of properties:

   | feels similar to silk | breathes like cotton | cheap | machine-washable | holds dye well |

3) The funding for the development of new materials often comes from manufacturing companies. This means research is often aimed at creating textiles they will find useful.

Smart Fabrics and Microfibres are Modern Materials

1) Smart fabrics change their properties in response to changes in their environment, e.g. they change shape or colour in response to changes in the temperature or light.
2) Microfibres were developed in the 1980s. They are very thin, fine fibres. They are made from other man-made fibres like rayon and nylon. Because they are so thin they can be woven into fabric very tightly. This close weave is very resistant to rain and wind — so microfibre fabric is often used for waterproof coats.

One day, this will be true. Just you wait.

The Materials used Change Over Time

The material used to make a particular product often changes over time. New materials with better properties replace the older materials used.

Example: women's swimming costumes

1) In the Victorian era women's swimsuits were very modest and made out of wool (serge or flannel).
2) In the 1930s swimsuits were made of cotton — it was more close-fitting and comfortable than wool and suited the feminine styles that were fashionable.
3) A new fabric called Lastex was invented in the 1930s. It was a stretchy fabric made from rubber. It was used to give swimsuits a more structured look in the 1940s and 1950s.
4) From the 1960s most swimsuits were made of a mixture of nylon and LYCRA®. These man-made fibres had properties which made them suitable. LYCRA® was stretchy and comfortable, nylon was strong and durable.

VELCRO® — fantastic for household fluff collection...

SOFTswitch™ fabrics are being developed — touch-sensitive fabrics which can act as an electronic switch. In the future you might never lose the TV remote because it'll be part of your sleeve.

Section 5 — Textiles

Processing Materials

Processes are all the things you can do to material to change it in some way. Anything from cutting and shaping to beetling and brushing to combining and strengthening to eating and spitting out...

Manufacturing Processes Improve Fabric Properties

Process	What it does
Beetling	Polishes and flattens the fabric by pressing it with rollers.
Brushing	Fabric is passed through a large rotating brush that raises the surface of the fabric. Brushing is used to make cotton softer for childrenswear.
Milling	Thickening and matting fabric by pressing and grinding it together.
Heat treatment	Synthetic fibres can be given 3D textures with heat treatment.
Chemical treatment	Chemicals can make fabrics resistant to creasing, fire, shrinking and water. They can also strengthen, stiffen, permanently crease or create other interesting effects, e.g. devoré is created by acid dissolving away bits of fabric.

Combining Fibres can Improve Fabric Properties

Combining fibres can be a cheap way to improve a fabric's properties, e.g. an expensive fibre and a cheap fibre can be mixed together to create an affordable fabric with an expensive texture.

1) A mixture fabric is made from two or more types of fibre.
   If the fabric is woven, the warp is one fibre and the weft is a different fibre,
   e.g. union fabric (for tea towels) is made from cotton and linen fibres.
2) A blended fabric is made from fibres which have been blended together before spinning into a thread,
   e.g. wool and cotton are blended to make Viyella®, which can then be made into fabric.

The Structure of Textiles can Improve their Properties

The properties of textiles are related to their structure. A weak fabric can be made into a strong garment if it has stitched pleats and strongly stitched seams.

Processes for Shaping and Structuring Materials

CUTTING — Fabric can be cut into shapes which fit the body nicely when sewn together.

TUCKS AND PLEATS — Fabric can be folded and either pressed or stitched, as a decorative way of removing fullness.

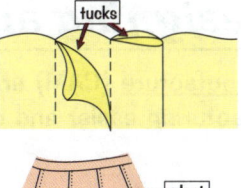

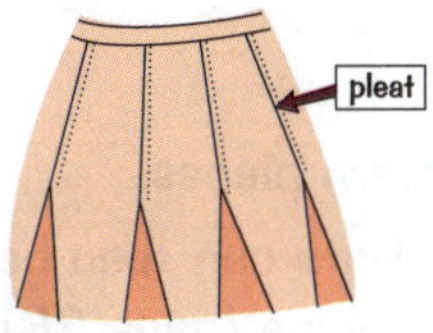

DARTS — A garment can be shaped by stitching away small triangular pieces of fabric.

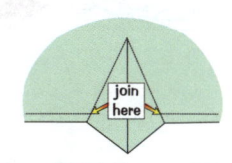

GATHERS — Similar to tucks and pleats, gathering is where a couple of rows of stitching are pulled to form small tucks.

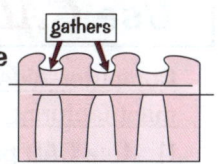

CORNERS — To strengthen corners, a second line of stitching can be added.

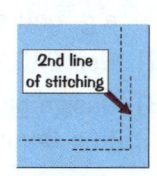

The Amazing Fibreman — with the powers of cotton and silk...

The properties of fabrics can be improved through manufacturing, combining fibres and textile structure, but not by eating and spitting out as it mentions in the intro — that was a fib, sorry.

Section 5 — Textiles

Techniques

Sew (get it) many beautiful techniques and so little time, so get a shifty on and learn this lot.

Patterns Help you Cut Fabric Accurately

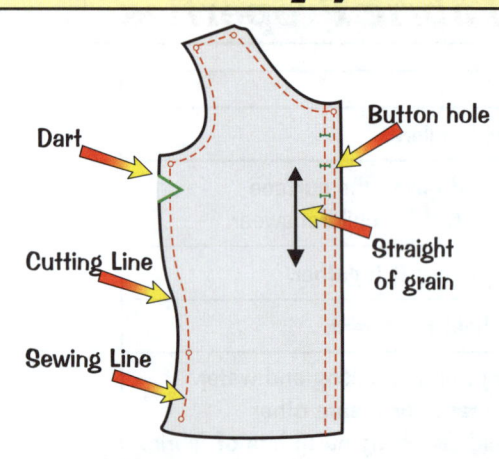

1) Patterns are templates you cut round. They're usually made of tissue paper, and you attach them to the material with pins.
2) A seam allowance is added to patterns so there is room to make a seam. It's the gap between the cutting line and the sewing line. It is normally 1.5 cm on a commercial pattern.
3) Symbols are used on patterns. They show where darts, button holes and the grain of the fabric go.

Decorating Techniques Personalise Products

1) Tie-dying — fabric is bunched and tied with string before it is dyed. This stops the dye from reaching some areas, resulting in different shaped patterns. This is a resist method of fabric decoration.
2) Batik — wax is drawn onto fabric with a special tool. The fabric is then dipped in dye and the wax resists the dye. The wax is then removed by ironing between absorbent paper. This is another resist method of decoration.
3) Fabric pens are used to draw onto fabric. The reverse of the fabric is ironed to fix the drawing in place.
4) Block printing is an old-fashioned method of decorating fabric. Shapes are stamped onto the fabric, e.g. potato printing.
5) Appliqué means cutting out shapes from fabric and sewing them onto a background fabric.
6) Stencilling is painting fabric dye through the holes of a stencil.

Fabric prepared for tie-dying

Appliqué

Design using fabric pens

Use CAD/CAM to Help with Designing and Making

Computer-Aided Design (CAD) and Computer-Aided Manufacture (CAM) are manufacturing aids — they make designing and manufacturing easier and quicker.

Read about CAD/CAM on page 14.

1) Use CAD programs to create designs on-screen, e.g. you can design patterns for embroidery.
2) Use CAD/CAM to design and produce stencils and pattern pieces.
3) Design blocks for block printing with a CAD package. Data can then be sent from the computer to a Computer Numerically Controlled (CNC) milling machine (page 26) — which will cut the blocks.

Dye tie dye — got it, I hated that tie...
I swear I never eat orange food. Yet it is there, on my right trouser leg. They come in the night you know, the ugly stain people, and laugh and laugh at me while I sleep. One day I will find them.

Section 5 — Textiles

47

More Techniques

Sewing machines use two threads. One is on a bobbin or spool under the sewing plate. The other (the top thread) is on a reel on top of the machine. The machine interlocks the two threads to make stitches.

Sewing Machines Vary — but the Basics are the Same

1) Make sure the machine is positioned so you can reach the machine and the foot pedal comfortably.
2) Choose the right needle for the work you're doing and fasten it securely into the machine.
3) Thread the top thread through the machine.
4) Place the bobbin into the machine. Then bring the bobbin thread through the sewing plate of the machine using the top thread and the balance wheel.
5) Check the tension of the threads is right. If the tension of the two threads is balanced then you will get an even stitch, which isn't too tight or too loose.
6) Select the right stitch type and length.
7) Turn the machine on at the mains.

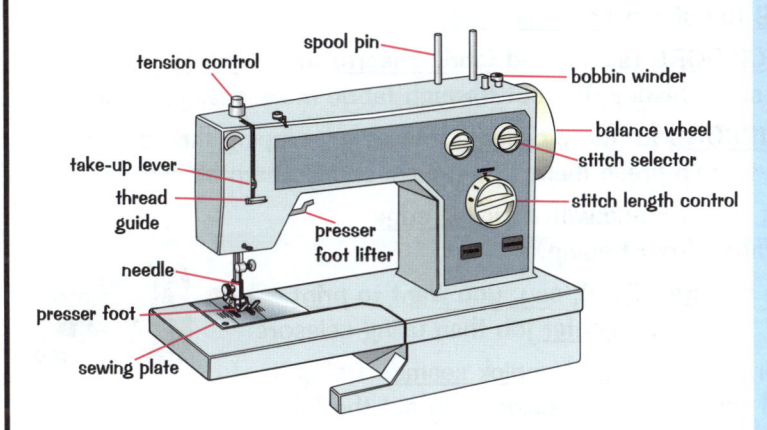

Sewing machine parts labelled: tension control, spool pin, bobbin winder, balance wheel, stitch selector, stitch length control, take-up lever, thread guide, presser foot lifter, needle, presser foot, sewing plate.

Tips for using sewing machines

1) Before you start on your main product, do some lines of stitching on a small sample of fabric. Check that the stitch type, stitch length and tension are right.
2) Tack fabric together using a simple hand stitch to hold a seam in place. After the seam has been stitched properly on the sewing machine the temporary stitch can be removed.
3) When you reach the end of a line of stitching, reverse the direction and sew back over the last 1 cm or so. This strengthens it.

Seams Join Pieces of Fabric Together

1) To make a flat seam, take two pieces of fabric and put the right sides together (the sides you want to be on the outside at the end).
2) Stitch the pieces together. Stitch about 1.5 cm in from the edge of the fabric (patterns have a seam allowance which gives extra fabric for this).
3) Open out the edges of the seam and iron them flat.
4) Turn the fabric the right way out — so the stitching is on the inside and there's a neat seam on the outside.

Flat seam — stitching

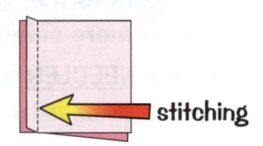

Curved seams
Cut notches into the edges of the fabric after you sew a curved seam — so that it will lie flat.
stitching, notches

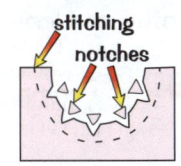

Corner seams
Stop at the corner, lower the needle using the balance wheel and lift the presser foot. Then turn the material around with the sewing machine needle still in the material. Then put the presser foot back down and carry on sewing in the new direction. To reduce bulk trim off the corner diagonally.
stitching

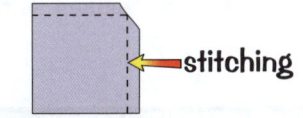

A stitch in thyme — makes a herb waistcoat...
There are loads of other types of seam, e.g. French seams, overlaid seams and piped seams.

Section 5 — Textiles

Tools and Equipment

There are lots of hand tools to get to grips with when you're manufacturing textiles products...

Use the Right Tools for the Job

FOR MARKING AND MEASURING

1) Use flexible MEASURING TAPES to accurately measure curved surfaces, e.g. a person's waist. 
2) Use TAILOR'S CHALK to transfer markings onto your fabric that you can remove later, e.g. when you're marking out a pattern.

FOR CUTTING

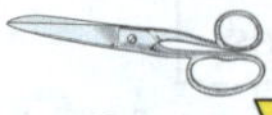

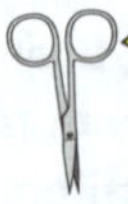

1) Use PAPER SCISSORS to cut out patterns.
2) Use DRESSMAKING SCISSORS (also called fabric shears) to cut fabric. These have long, very sharp blades that cut through fabric more easily and neatly.
3) Use EMBROIDERY SCISSORS for more delicate jobs, e.g. snipping threads, or clipping curved seams to help press them. They have short, sharp blades.
4) Use PINKING SHEARS to cut fabric with a zigzag edge — this helps prevent fabric from fraying.
5) Use CRAFT KNIVES to cut stencils (if, say, you want to print a design onto fabric). You'll do a neater job than using scissors. 
6) Use SEAM RIPPERS or UNPICKERS to unpick seams. Doing it by hand is slower, and scissors might accidentally cut the fabric.

FOR SEWING

1) Use PINS to hold the fabric together before stitching with a sewing machine. Doing this means the fabric won't slip, and you can keep your fingers further away from the needle when you feed fabric through. (For more safety tips, see p. 27.) 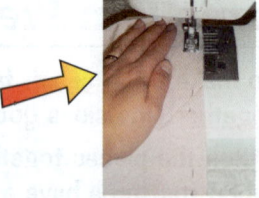
2) Use NEEDLES for hand stitching, e.g. embroidery, attaching beads to fabric, or tacking.
3) Use a needle that's the right size for the thickness of the fabric and the thread you're using.

FOR PRESSING

1) DRY IRONS use heat and pressure to press creases out of fabric and flatten seams.
2) STEAM IRONS are more effective — they use water and steam as well as heat and pressure.

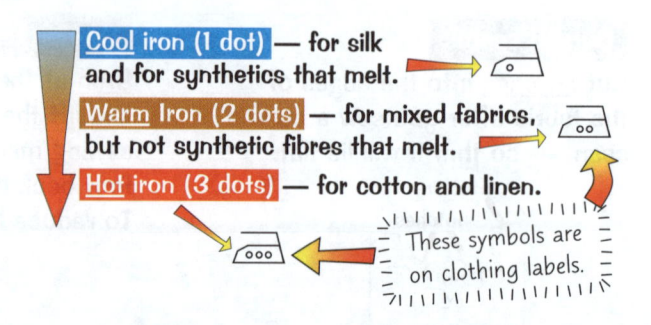

Cool iron (1 dot) — for silk and for synthetics that melt.
Warm Iron (2 dots) — for mixed fabrics, but not synthetic fibres that melt.
Hot iron (3 dots) — for cotton and linen.

These symbols are on clothing labels.

Sewing — it seamed like a good idea at the time...

When it comes to textiles, this page shows you the tools of the trade... literally. So make sure you know all about them, including what they look like and why particular ones are suited to certain jobs.

Section 5 — Textiles

Section 6 — Cooking and Nutrition

Nutrition

To be healthy, you need to make sure the food you eat contains all the nutrients your body needs to work properly. Make sure you know what does what and what's in what...

Different Foods Contain Different Nutrients

1) There are five nutrients that are vital to health — proteins, fats, carbohydrates, vitamins and minerals.
2) These nutrients can be split into two groups — macronutrients and micronutrients.

Macronutrients
Macro means large — we need macronutrients in large amounts.

CARBOHYDRATES — for ENERGY

1) Carbohydrates provide the body with energy. Carbohydrates include sugars and starches.
2) Biscuits and cakes are good sources of sugar. Bread, pasta and potatoes are all high in starch.

PROTEIN — for GROWTH

1) Protein is needed by the body to grow new cells and repair old and damaged cells.
2) Meat, fish, cheese, eggs, beans, lentils and nuts are all good sources of protein.

FATS — for ENERGY

1) Fat supplies the body with energy and some vitamins (A, D, E and K).
2) Sources include butter, lard, olive oil, nuts and pastries.

Micronutrients
Micro means small — we need micronutrients in much smaller amounts.

VITAMINS — There are lots of different vitamins you need to keep healthy. For example:

1) Vitamin A is good for vision, especially when it's dark. You can find it in fish, eggs, butter, oranges and dark green vegetables.
2) Vitamin C is used to help your body fight disease and absorb iron. Oranges, peppers, tomatoes, green vegetables and (slightly surprisingly) potatoes all contain vitamin C.

MINERALS — There are lots of minerals you need to eat to stay healthy. Just like vitamins, the body uses different minerals to do different things. For example:

1) Iron is needed to make red blood cells. Iron is in foods such as red meat and green vegetables.
2) Calcium's needed for strong bones. It's found in foods such as milk, cheese and green vegetables.

You also Need Plenty of Water and Fibre

1) Fibre isn't digested by the body but it helps make your body's digestive system work properly. It's found in foods such as vegetables, wholemeal bread and beans.
2) Water is needed for lots of things in your body. For example, keeping you at the right temperature and digesting your food. It's found in all drinks and lots of foods, such as fruit and vegetables.

Different people have different nutritional needs...

For example an elderly person will probably need less protein and carbohydrate than an energetic teenager because they're not growing or running about quite as much. Makes sense really when you think about it.

Healthy Eating

Healthy eating means getting the right balance of nutrients from your diet (the food you eat).

It's Important to Have a Healthy Diet

Having too much or too little of some nutrients can lead to health problems. A healthy diet should be:

- low in fat, especially saturated fat
- low in sugar
- low in salt
- high in fibre
- varied — eating lots of different foods means you're more likely to get all the nutrients you need.

Use the Eatwell Plate to Check Your Diet is Right

The eatwell plate is a way of showing how much of each type of food you should eat:

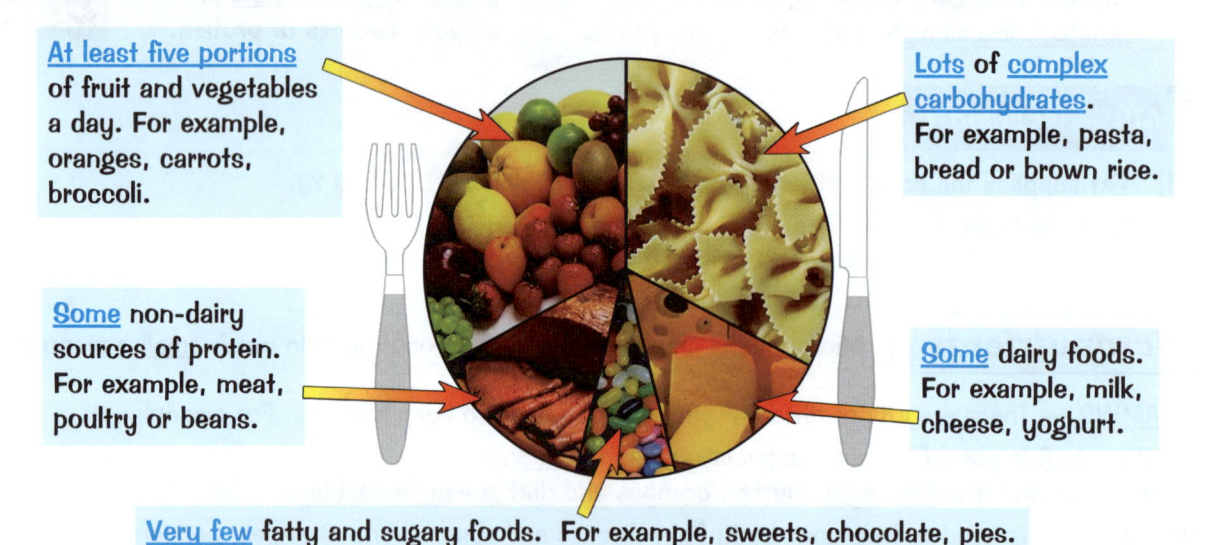

- **At least five portions** of fruit and vegetables a day. For example, oranges, carrots, broccoli.
- **Lots** of complex carbohydrates. For example, pasta, bread or brown rice.
- **Some** non-dairy sources of protein. For example, meat, poultry or beans.
- **Some** dairy foods. For example, milk, cheese, yoghurt.
- **Very few** fatty and sugary foods. For example, sweets, chocolate, pies.

If Your Diet is Unhealthy, You May Become Obese

1) Eating too many carbohydrates, fatty foods or sugary foods can lead to obesity (being overweight).
2) This is because these foods are high in energy. If you take in more energy than your body uses up, then the spare energy is stored as fat.
3) Obesity increases the risk of developing type 2 diabetes, high blood pressure, heart disease and some forms of cancer.
4) Other foods cause problems too. For example, eating too much salty food can cause high blood pressure, and too much fat can cause high cholesterol.

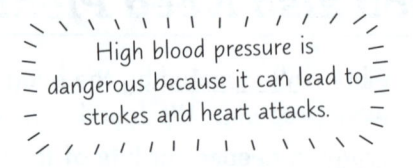

High blood pressure is dangerous because it can lead to strokes and heart attacks.

You need to eat well to be healthy...

Not eating well can lead to loads of health problems. Having a healthy diet doesn't mean you need to cut out fatty and sugary foods like cake altogether, you've just got to make sure you have them as part of a balanced and varied diet. And no, eating a different cake each day doesn't count as a varied diet...

Section 6 — Cooking and Nutrition

Selecting Ingredients

Ingredients are all very different — it matters big time what you decide to put in your recipe.
If you run out of milk, it's no good throwing in something else from a cow — like a leather jacket.

Choose Ingredients with Properties that Suit Your Product

There are several things to think about when choosing ingredients:

1) Function — some ingredients do a useful job, e.g. self-raising flour joins everything together and gives a recipe bulk, but it also makes products light and airy.
2) Nutritional values — some ingredients provide important nutrients, e.g. cheese provides protein and flour provides carbohydrate and minerals.
3) Specialist diets — some ingredients aren't suitable for people with e.g. diabetes or coeliac disease.
4) Aesthetic properties — how the ingredients look, feel, smell and taste, e.g. desiccated coconut crust provides texture, makes the crust crisp and adds flavour.
5) Cost — whether the ingredients are affordable.
6) Shelf-life — how long the ingredients will last before they deteriorate.
7) Availability — if it is possible to buy the ingredients locally, in the amounts needed.
8) Environmental and ethical issues — you may prefer to use foods which are organically grown, free-range, vegetarian or fair-traded.

You Have to Compromise When Selecting Ingredients

1) It's often difficult to find ingredients that have all the properties and characteristics you are looking for, e.g. ingredients which have the right taste, smell and look may be expensive or not easily available.
2) You often have to compromise when selecting ingredients. Decide which properties and characteristics are most important for your product and choose an ingredient that has those.

Healthy Eating Guidelines are Increasingly Important

1) A healthy diet is important — the public is becoming more aware of the risk of diet-related diseases, such as heart disease and some cancers.
2) Food designers should aim to create foods which give the consumer a healthy choice.
3) In order to increase the 'healthiness' of a food, five things need to be focused on:

INCREASING FIBRE CONTENT
e.g. using wholegrain products or using raw or lightly cooked vegetables or fruits.

INCREASING FRUIT AND VEGETABLE CONTENT
— so the product helps you on the way to eating at least 5 portions a day.

REDUCING SALT-CONTENT
e.g. avoiding adding salt to food, using low-salt alternatives to bacon and other salt-cured products.

REDUCING SUGAR CONTENT
e.g. replacing some of the sugar with dried fruit (which has a concentrated sweet flavour but fewer calories).

REDUCING FAT CONTENT
e.g. using low-fat alternatives or reducing the proportion of fat in the recipe.

Want a cake with less fat? Try a smaller one...

Think about all the different factors when choosing ingredients, and decide what's most important when you're making your product. Oh and you might want to go easy on the sugar-coated, salty lard cakes — OK.

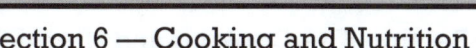

Section 6 — Cooking and Nutrition

Properties of Ingredients

Different ingredients have different properties — lemon's great for keeping fruit fresh and eggs are great for throwing at bad politicians. These properties affect what happens when you process them.

Ingredients Have Useful Properties

1) Protein Foods (things like eggs, nuts, meat and cheese)
Eggs are great for loads of reasons —

- Eggs set (coagulate) when heated, which gives strength to a product.
- Eggs can be added to sauces to help thicken them when heated gently. 
- Egg whites can be whisked to create a foam, which makes products light and fluffy.
- Egg yolk contains an emulsifier (lecithin), which holds oil and water together when they want to pull apart, e.g. in mayonnaise.

2) Carbohydrate Foods

Flour (a starchy carbohydrate)
- Flour adds texture and structure.
- Flour can be used to thicken sauces (gelatinisation) by absorbing the liquid in the sauce and making a gel.

Sugary carbohydrates
- Sugary carbohydrates sweeten foods.
- Sugary carbohydrates caramelise with heat to thicken food and add flavour.

Fibre
- Fibre found in carbohydrate foods helps to give products bulk.
- Fibre absorbs liquid added to the product and makes it bigger and easier to digest.

3) Fatty Foods

- Fatty foods in general add flavour, as well as colour and texture.
- Butter gives pastry a nice flavour and lard helps to shorten the pastry (by surrounding the flour particles) — this gives the pastry a nice crumbly texture.

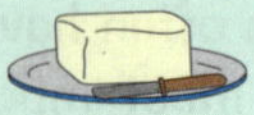

Processing Changes the Structure of Food

1) The structure of ingredients depends on whether they are meat, vegetables or processed food.
2) Meat and vegetables still have their original cell structure. This often makes them quite tough, and they need to be softened by cooking.
3) Processed foods have a more complicated structure. They are often made up of two ingredients mixed together. Examples include:
   - Foams — air (or another gas) mixed with a liquid, e.g. whipped cream.
   - Emulsions — water and oil mixed together and held together by an emulsifier, e.g. mayonnaise.
   - Suspensions — a solid held in a liquid, e.g. custard.
   - Gels — a small amount of solid used to set a lot of liquid, e.g. jam.
4) You can use different processes to achieve a particular structure. E.g. aerating a food product to make a foam can be done:
   - Physically, e.g. whisking egg white into a foam.
   - Chemically, e.g. using a raising agent like bicarbonate of soda.
   - Biologically, e.g. yeast is used to make dough rise.

Plain, self-raising and wholemeal — a bunch of flours...

Chickens just don't get enough credit for laying eggs. Their eggs can coagulate, emulsify, be whisked, scrambled, thicken sauces... And then what do chickens get in return? Eaten, that's what.

Section 6 — Cooking and Nutrition

Modern Ingredients

In times gone by, gruel might have ruled. But thankfully things are different now.

Scientific Developments Mean New Ingredients

1) Scientists have developed new ingredients with new properties.
2) This means designers can create food products that weren't possible before.
3) Research into new ingredients is often focused on particular needs, e.g. low-fat alternatives or vegetarian alternatives. This is because research is often funded by manufacturers. They want ingredients to be developed which they will find useful in their products.

Examples Include GM Foods and Modified Starches

1) **GENETICALLY MODIFIED (GM) FOODS** Scientists have changed the genes of some plants.
Genes control what a plant is like and how it grows. Foods that have been changed in this way are called genetically modified (GM) foods. Many people don't agree with improving crops this way (see page 28). E.g. Scientists have found the gene in tomatoes that's responsible for ripening — and tried replacing it with one that makes them ripen more slowly (so they have a longer shelf-life).

2) **MODIFIED STARCHES** Modified starches have been altered to react to different environments.
In food technology they're called smart starches. E.g. pre-gelatinised starch thickens instantly when mixed with hot water. It's used in packet custard and Pot Noodles.

3) **FUNCTIONAL FOODS** These foods have health benefits.
E.g. bio-yoghurts which contain live bacteria to aid digestion.

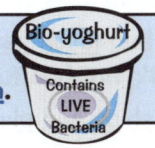

4) **NUTRACEUTICALS** These are foods that have been developed to help solve particular problems.
E.g. fats and dairy produce containing special ingredients to help lower cholesterol — which lowers the risk of heart disease.

5) **NOVEL FOODS** These are completely new foods that have been developed to meet a need.
E.g. Quorn™ is a vegetarian alternative to meat, made of mycoprotein (protein from fungi). It's often used where you'd normally use chicken. It's available in different sizes, e.g. chunks for stir fries, or mince for bolognese sauce. Quorn™ doesn't taste of much, so is often flavoured or marinated (soaked in a sauce).

I won't touch GM foods and I'm a goat-pig-dog-carrot...

It's all very easy to make GM food gags, but just because it's relatively new and it involves people in white coats, it doesn't mean it's immediately bad. (P.S. If they can make a buttered-crumpet plant, I'm in).

Section 6 — Cooking and Nutrition

Sourcing Ingredients

Your food doesn't just magically appear in the supermarket — some of it's travelled thousands of miles.

A Lot of Food Made in the UK Isn't Available All the Time

1) Most fruits and vegetables grown in the UK are available to buy at different times of the year — they are seasonal.
2) A food is in season when it's ready to be harvested.
3) Different foods are in season for different lengths of time. For example:

Food	When it's in season
Aubergine	June – October
Apples	October – December
Leeks	September – March
Carrots	May – October

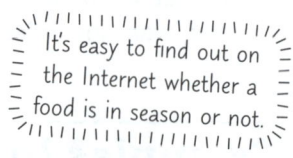

It's easy to find out on the Internet whether a food is in season or not.

4) It's not just fruit and vegetables that are seasonal and vary in availability — different types of meat, poultry, game and seafood in the UK are seasonal too. E.g. lamb is in season during the spring.
5) Some processed foods are also only available at certain times of year because they're linked to a particular celebration. E.g. hot cross buns and Easter eggs are only available around Easter.

A Lot of the Food We Eat Was Grown in Other Countries

1) People want to be able to buy foods all year round, not just when they're in season in the UK.
2) Shops buy food from abroad when it's out of season at home. They also buy things from abroad that just can't be grown here, like bananas.
3) It's best to buy local, seasonal produce if you can. Food grown locally will be fresher — it's not had to travel for as long to get from the producer to the shop.
4) The lorries, ships and planes used to transport food burn fossil fuels, which is bad for the environment. The further food has to be transported, the more fossil fuels get burnt and the more polluted the environment becomes.

We bring it, you eat it...

You Might Need to Shop Around to Find Ingredients

1) Large supermarkets sell a lot of different types of food — you should be able to find most of the food you need there.
2) For more unusual ingredients you may need to go to specialist stores, e.g. Chinese supermarkets.
3) Farmers' markets are a good source of local, seasonal products. The food is often fresher than the food in supermarkets.

Onions are so in this season...

Urgh, imagine what it was like before we started importing food — you'd only be able to get a tasty apple three months of the year. Thankfully you can have pretty much any food you like whenever you like now, but food is most likely to be at its freshest and tastiest when it's grown locally and in season.

Section 6 — Cooking and Nutrition

Additives

There are ways of improving food products so they're nicer than ever — mmm, read on...

Additives are Really Useful Substances Added to Food

1) An additive is something that's added to a food product to improve its properties.
2) Additives have loads of different uses — from improving taste to extending shelf life.
3) Some additives are natural (made from plants/animals) and some are made artificially.
4) All additives must pass a safety test before they can be used in food. When an additive passes it gets an E number, meaning it can be used throughout the European Union, e.g. caramel colouring is E150a.

Seasoning Food Makes it Taste Better

1) Flavourings are one type of additive — they improve the taste or the smell of a product.
2) Adding flavourings to food is called 'seasoning'.
3) The key to seasoning is to just keep tasting and sniffing your food while you add your seasoning a bit at a time. That way you'll be able to tell when you've got your food tasting just right and avoid putting too much in.
4) The most common flavourings we add to food are good ol' salt and pepper.
5) Herbs and spices are natural flavourings — they improve the taste, e.g. adding basil makes tomato-flavoured pasta sauces more tasty, and chillies add spice to a range of foods. Using dried herbs and spices gives a slightly different flavour to using fresh ones.
6) Vanilla flavouring can be natural (from vanilla pods) or artificial (vanillin solution). It's used in lots of cakes and desserts, e.g. vanilla-flavoured ice-cream.

Preservatives (Unsurprisingly) Preserve Food

Preservatives are additives that make food last for longer.
For example:

- Vinegar is used to pickle foods like onions and eggs.
- Salt is used to cure meat, e.g. ham, bacon.
- The sugar in jam preserves the fruit in it.

Colourings Can be Used to Make Food Look Nicer

1) Colourings are additives that make food look more attractive and more appealing to eat.
2) They can be used to add colour to something colourless, or to return food to its natural colour if it's lost during processing.
3) For example, the peas used to make mushy peas lose some of their colour when they've been cooked long enough to go mushy, so tinned mushy peas often contain food colourings to make them look greener.

There's more on food processing on p.57.

I'd like a vanilla-flavoured rainbow-coloured egg please...

Unless you grow everything you eat (unlikely), you'll probably be gobbling up a fair few additives — they're just so darn useful. So make sure you know why they're useful, and learn some examples too.

Section 6 — Cooking and Nutrition

Processing Ingredients

Processing food can improve taste and texture, kill bacteria or increase shelf-life — nice one. Unfortunately it also destroys many of the fantastically healthy nutrients in raw food — doh!

Processing Can Make Food Taste Better and Last Longer

1) Food can be eaten raw, or it can be processed before we eat it. Processing means changing the food, e.g. by mashing, cooking, combining ingredients, adding preservatives or adding colourings.

2) Heat treatment (cooking) is one of the most common processing methods. There are lots of ways you can heat food — boiling in a liquid, steaming, frying with fat, roasting, grilling and baking. Different heat treatments have different results, e.g. fried eggs look and taste different to boiled eggs.

3) Using different processes you can produce very different meals from the same ingredients. E.g. in a sauce recipe, you stir and gently heat eggs to thicken the sauce and make it smooth. In another recipe, using the same ingredients, you separate out the egg whites and whisk them to make a foam, fold the foam into the sauce, then bake the mixture to get a light airy soufflé.

Varying the *Proportions* of Ingredients Has a Big Effect

1) Combining ingredients together produces different flavours, textures and smells.
2) Similar ingredients used in different proportions can give you very different results, e.g. in making pastry —

Rich Shortcrust Pastry
200g plain flour
100g margarine/butter
2 eggs
50g caster sugar
pinch of salt

Shortcrust Pastry
200g plain flour
100g margarine/lard
2 tablespoons cold water
pinch of salt

Flaky Pastry
200g plain flour
150g butter/lard
pinch salt
2 teaspoons lemon juice
8 tablespoons cold water

Forming and Cutting Food Makes it Look Good

1) Forming a product simply means shaping it, e.g. shaping minced beef into patties to make burgers.
2) Forming can be done using moulds, e.g. Christmas pudding, jelly and angel cakes are cooked or set in moulds.
3) Cutting is just what you'd expect — using some kind of blade to chop up the product.
4) Cutting doesn't just mean knives — it could also include things like a shape cutter, e.g. a star-shaped cutter for Christmas biscuits.
5) Shaping food makes the final dish look more attractive.

Good things come to those who weigh...

Your product has got to taste great AND look good too. If your tasty pasta dish looks like maggots on a cow-pat with side order of sick, it's not going to sell — you have to entice people with how it looks.

Section 6 — Cooking and Nutrition

Food Processing

You can eat some food, e.g. apples, totally raw. But a lot of food needs to be changed in some way before it's nice to eat. Chicken for example — the feathers, claws and bones get stuck in your throat.

There are Four Main Food Processing Techniques

Most of the food we eat requires some processing before we can eat it — e.g. potatoes are peeled and cooked before they are edible.

Processing can either be primary or secondary.

PRIMARY PROCESSING — taking raw ingredients and changing them into an edible form or into an ingredient that can be made into another product.
E.g. Wheat ➡ Flour

SECONDARY PROCESSING — taking foods that have already been processed and changing them into another product.
E.g. Flour ➡ Bread

There are four main food processing techniques:

1. Mechanical, e.g. harvesting, cleaning
2. Heat, e.g. pasteurisation, freezing, baking, frying
3. Chemical, e.g. salting, pickling
4. Irradiation — exposing food to radiation that will kill bacteria and extend the shelf-life of the food.

Milk is pasteurised.

Processing and combining ingredients changes their characteristics and properties, e.g.

Boiling vegetables dissolves away or destroys some vitamins — so they lose some of their nutritious properties.

Flour contains gluten. When it is combined with a liquid, it gains new properties, becoming stretchy and elastic.

Different Equipment Gives Different Results

1) Using different equipment to process food gives different results — e.g. different textures.
2) When designing new food products, designers often experiment with different equipment.

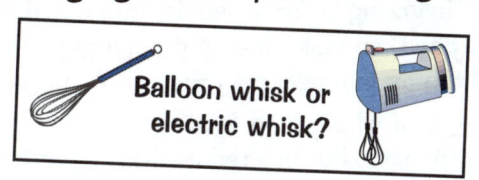

- Balloon whisk or electric whisk?
- Blender or wooden spoon?
- Kitchen knives or food processors?
- Oven or microwave?

More on cooking and equipment coming up on pages 59–63.

3) The equipment used isn't the only thing which affects results — altering the cooking method can change things too, e.g. baked, boiled and fried potatoes have different flavours and textures.

What's red, green, red, green? — a frog in a blender...

Don't let the term 'food processing' confuse you. It's not just something done by a machine with a scary whizzing blade, it's pretty much anything you do to change food — cooking, cleaning, peeling, juggling...

Section 6 — Cooking and Nutrition

Planning a Meal

Unless you're very rich or a celebrity with a personal chef, you're going to need to be able to make healthy, tasty meals to feed yourself and anyone else you might want to. Read on...

Your Diet Needs to be Nutritionally Balanced

1) Meals should be nutritionally balanced. They should contain a mixture of vegetables, carbohydrates and protein (see page 50).
2) When making a meal for someone, you should find out if they have any special dietary requirements. For example:
   - Vegetarians don't eat meat, so you can't make them steak for dinner.
   - Some people are allergic or intolerant to certain foods, e.g. nuts, dairy etc. 
3) Some people just don't like certain foods, so it's best to check whether anyone has any particular likes or dislikes. That way you won't end up serving sprout soup to a sprout hater.
4) Meals also need to be tasty and look nice. Otherwise you, your family and friends just aren't going to want to eat them, no matter how good they are for you.

1) A good meal should provide food with a variety of colour, texture and flavour.
2) Colourful foods look more appealing than white or brown foods.
3) Different flavours that go well together should be combined in a dish. For example, a spicy curry with a mild yoghurt dip.
4) Different textures make food appealing. For example, a meal of mince, mashed potato and mushy peas might not be that appealing because all the food is sloppy.

Adapt and Invent Your Own Recipes to Suit Your Needs

Recipes can help you create tasty meals, but don't be afraid to adapt them or make up your own recipes from scratch — whatever works best for you.

1) If a recipe uses ingredients that are expensive or out of season, you could just leave them out or swap them for something that's in season or cheaper.
2) If you're making a meal for two, but the recipe you're following is for 4 people, you could reduce the amount of each ingredient you use (in this case by half) to make the right amount of food. You might also need to reduce the cooking time a bit too as the meal may then cook quicker.
3) You can adapt recipes to match the dietary requirements of who you're feeding. E.g. If someone's on a low fat diet, you could cook with less oil or use reduced-fat ingredients.
4) You can also adapt recipes just to match your personal taste. If you hate a particular ingredient, then don't use it. If you love a particular ingredient, you could try adding it to a recipe.
5) Changing an ingredient might change the food you're making, e.g. it might add more moisture and make a mixture more runny. You might then need to add or change other ingredients to make the recipe still work, e.g. add a bit of flour to soak up the extra liquid.

Bacon and haddock cake wasn't my finest recipe idea...

Adapting recipes is fun and useful. If you don't like the main ingredient in a recipe though, then it's probably best just not to use that recipe, e.g. you can't really make an omelette without eggs. But otherwise pretty much anything goes — release your inner Heston and see what delicious creations you can come up with.

Section 6 — Cooking and Nutrition

Cooking Methods

Different <u>cooking methods</u> are used to cook different <u>types of food</u>. Here are some of the common ones...

You can Cook Food Using Hot Liquids

Boiling

Add food to boiling water carefully so that it doesn't splash.

1) <u>Boiling</u> means cooking food in <u>boiling liquid</u>, usually <u>water</u>. You can tell water is boiling by the <u>large</u>, <u>fast moving bubbles</u>.
2) <u>Vegetables</u>, <u>rice</u> and <u>pasta</u> are often boiled.
3) Boiling makes the <u>texture</u> of food <u>softer</u>. If food is boiled for too long it'll get too soft.
4) Boiling is usually <u>quick</u> and <u>simple</u>, and <u>no fat</u> is added so it's <u>healthy</u> too.
5) Vegetables can lose some <u>vitamins</u> and <u>minerals</u> during boiling though, so try and boil vegetables for the <u>shortest time</u> possible.

Simmering and Poaching

1) <u>Simmering</u> and <u>poaching</u> food is basically the same as boiling it — the only difference is the <u>temperature</u> of the water.
2) Simmering is more <u>gentle</u> than boiling — the liquid used is heated to a <u>lower temperature</u> and the <u>bubbles</u> in the liquid are <u>smaller</u>. <u>Fewer nutrients</u> are lost when a food is <u>simmered</u> rather than <u>boiled</u>.
3) <u>Soups</u> and <u>stews</u> (see below) are usually simmered.
4) <u>Poaching</u> means cooking food <u>very gently</u> in hot liquid that has not reached a simmer.
5) Poaching is used to cook <u>delicate</u> foods, like <u>eggs</u> and <u>fish</u>. If foods like this were boiled they would <u>break apart</u>.

Cooking foods using liquids help keep food moist.

Steaming

1) <u>Steaming</u> means cooking food with <u>steam</u> from boiling water.
2) Steaming food helps to <u>preserve</u> its <u>colour</u>, <u>texture</u> and <u>vitamins</u>.
3) Foods you can steam include <u>fish</u>, <u>vegetables</u> and <u>rice</u>.

Stewing and Braising

1) <u>Stewing</u> means cooking food <u>slowly</u> in its <u>own juices</u> or in a <u>stock</u>.
2) It's often used to cook <u>tough meat</u>, such as cheap cuts of beef.
3) The slow and gentle cooking in liquid makes the meat <u>tender</u>.
4) The cooking liquid becomes a <u>sauce</u> for the food.
5) <u>Braising</u> is like stewing, but the food is usually <u>fried</u> (see next page) to <u>brown</u> it first.

What a steamy page...

Hot water is really useful for cooking food — you can vary the <u>temperature</u> of the water depending on how <u>delicate</u> the food is, and it's <u>healthy</u> (as long as you don't let too many of the nutrients in the food escape into the water). There are some foods which don't taste that great just heated up in some water though, and boiled meat doesn't really look great. Thankfully there are other ways to cook food, huzzah...

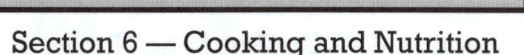

Section 6 — Cooking and Nutrition

Cooking Methods

This page is all about how to fry and microwave food. Frying means cooking food in hot fat. Mmm...

You Can Use Fat to Fry Food

1) Frying uses fat or oil heated to a very high temperature to cook food quickly.
2) The food absorbs fat as it cooks. This adds flavour, but makes the food less healthy.
3) The fat should be hot. This stops the food absorbing too much oil and going soggy.
4) There are a few different frying methods:

Safety is important. Avoid splashing the hot oil and avoid mixing water with oil (or you'll make it spit).

Shallow Frying

1) Shallow frying uses a frying pan and a medium amount of oil.
2) Foods that can be shallow-fried include fish, meat and eggs.
3) Most foods need turning so they brown on both sides.

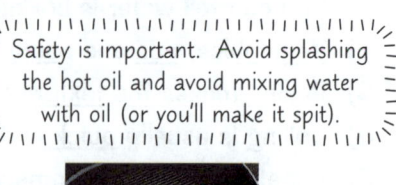

Deep-Fat Frying

1) In deep-fat frying, food is completely submerged in very hot oil.
2) Delicate foods (like fish) are often dipped in batter (a water and flour mix) before frying. The batter absorbs fat and goes crispy, while the food inside stays moist.
3) Foods that can be deep fried include fish, chips and doughnuts.

Stir-Frying

1) Stir-frying uses a wok and a little hot oil. It's healthier than shallow frying.
2) The food should be chopped up small so it cooks quickly. It also needs to be moved around all the time so it doesn't burn.
3) Stir-frying is popular because:
   - it's quick — the food cooks very fast
   - it combines ingredients with different colours and textures (for example, peppers, spring onions, beansprouts and meat).
4) Stir-fried foods include Asian dishes like stir-fried noodles and vegetable stir-fry.

Microwaving is a Quick, Easy Way to Cook Many Foods

1) Microwaves heat up the water, fat and sugars in food to cook it.
2) They're mostly used for defrosting and reheating pre-prepared foods.
3) They're popular because they cook food really quickly and are easy to use.
4) It's not safe to use metal dishes in a microwave, because they'll spark.
5) Normal microwaves don't brown food, so they can make some foods soggy.

Mmmm frying...

All the best foods are fried... chips, doughnuts, more chips... but it's important that you don't eat lots of fried foods. Frying is less healthy than most of the other methods in this book because you need to add fat. To make sure you have a varied and healthy diet, you should only eat fried food occasionally and use as little fat as possible when you fry food yourself. Next up, another tasty set of cooking methods...

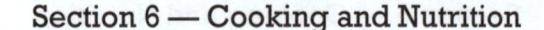

Section 6 — Cooking and Nutrition

Cooking Methods

Right, that's all the cooking with fat, water and microwaves done with. Just dry heat to go...

You can use Dry Heat to Cook Food

1) Dry heat means cooking foods without using liquids. You might want to apply a bit of fat to some foods being cooked this way to help stop them drying out.
2) The most common cooking methods that use dry heat (see below) use an oven or a grill.
3) Ovens heat the air inside the oven until it's reached a particular temperature. Food placed in the oven will be heated by the hot air in the oven.
4) Electric grills have a heating element (thick bit of wire) that gets very hot and heats the food below it. Gas grills use a flame to heat food.

Baking

1) Baked foods are cooked in an oven.
2) The outside of baked foods goes brown and crisp.
3) Baking foods like potatoes and fish is healthier than frying or roasting because no extra fat is added.
4) Food can dry out during baking. Foods like fish and chicken can be baked in foil parcels to keep them moist.
5) Foods that are often baked include bread, pastries, cakes, potatoes and fish.

Roasting

1) Roasted food is also cooked in an oven.
2) Fat is added to the outside of roasted food. This helps the outside to go brown and crisp, while the inside stays moist.
3) Large cuts of meat (like a joint of beef or lamb or a whole chicken) are very popular roasted. Vegetables (like potatoes and parsnips) can be roasted too.

Grilling

1) Grilling cooks food at a very high temperature. Because the heat is so high the food cooks quickly and browns on the outside.
2) It's fairly healthy because no fat is added, and fat drips out of the food as it cooks.
3) The high heat can make it hard to cook the food evenly. It's easy to burn the food, or to end up with the outside cooked but the inside still raw.
4) Grilling can be used to cook tender meat, fish and vegetables.
5) Barbecuing is a type of grilling where food is cooked outside over hot coals. This gives barbecued food a nice smoky flavour.

My mum gives me a grilling all the time...

...sadly it's less about steak and more about what a bombsite my room is. Oh well. There are lots of different ways to cook food — we've just covered the main ones here. Make sure you know what each cooking method is, which foods are good to cook using each method and how healthy each one is.

Section 6 — Cooking and Nutrition

Cooking Equipment

You can't chop a carrot with a spoon, and you can't scoop up soup with a fork... well you could try, but you wouldn't get very far. Making meals is a lot easier when you use the right tools for the job.

Preparing Food is Easy with the Right Equipment

You could fill a whole book with all the wonderful kitchen tools and gadgets you can use to transform a bunch of ingredients into a tasty meal. Here are a few of the basics...

Knives are Used for Chopping and Slicing

1) The main tools you'll use for chopping and slicing are knives.
2) The bigger and tougher the bit of food you're cutting up, the bigger your knife should be. It's important to use sharp knives so they cut food easily.
3) Serrated knives have a jagged edge, which makes them really useful for cutting soft foods with a harder outer layer, e.g. crusty bread.

Spoons and Whisks Can be Used to Mix and Whip Ingredients

WHISKS

1) Balloon whisk — for whisking or whipping, for example egg whites or cream.
2) Spiral whisk — for mixing and preventing lumps forming in sauces.

balloon whisk   spiral whisk

SPOONS

1) Wooden spoon — for stirring, mixing and beating ingredients together, e.g. when making a cake. Wooden spoons also don't heat up easily, which makes them really useful for stirring hot food without burning your hand.  
2) Metal spoon — for mixing and folding ingredients together. Folding is used to gently combine ingredients, e.g. whisked egg whites are often folded into a cake mixture to keep as much of the air in the mixture as possible (if too much is lost, the cake won't rise). Metal spoons can also be used to measure ingredients (see next page).

You Need Tools for Spreading, Scraping and Scooping

Knives and spoons can be used to spread, scoop and scrape ingredients. There are some other (and sometimes more useful) pieces of equipment you can use to do this too:

1) Spatulas have a bendy head which means they can get right against the side of a container. This makes them great for scraping mixtures from bowls and pans.
2) Palette knives are blunt, flexible knives with a rounded tip. They're used for scraping, spreading and mixing ingredients. Palette knives can also be used to lift and turn food during cooking.
3) Ladles are spoons with a long handle that can hold a lot of liquid. They're useful tools for adding stock to a dish or serving food, e.g. soup.

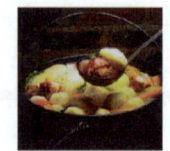

Spoons also make a great musical instrument...

This is all pretty basic stuff, but if you don't know what the best tool for a job is, you're just going to make life hard for yourself. Before you start making a meal, make sure you've got the equipment you need.

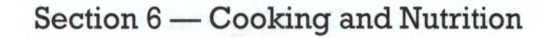

Section 6 — Cooking and Nutrition

Cooking Equipment

Couldn't get enough of cooking equipment? That's lucky, here's another page on the lovely stuff...

Measuring Ingredients is Important

It's important if you're following a recipe to make sure you measure out all your ingredients correctly. If you don't, the balance of ingredients in your dish won't be right, which will probably lead to the finished meal not looking or tasting as nice. E.g. If you don't get the balance of flour, fat, sugar and eggs right in a cake mix, the cake may not rise or taste very nice.

You need to use different things to measure different amounts/ingredients. For example:

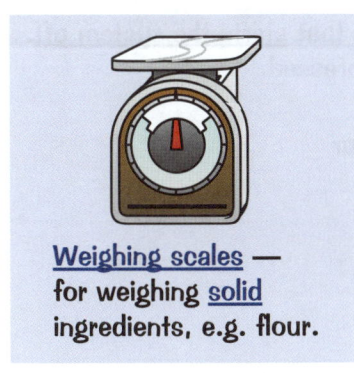

Weighing scales — for weighing solid ingredients, e.g. flour.

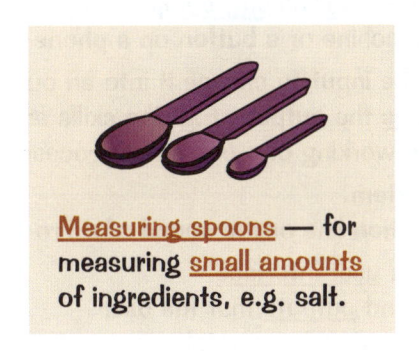

Measuring spoons — for measuring small amounts of ingredients, e.g. salt.

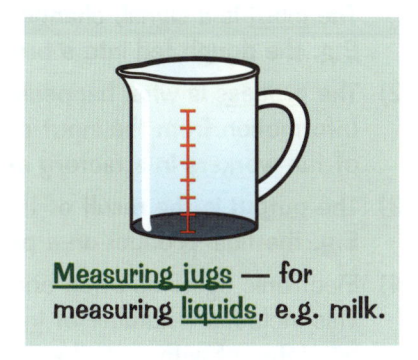

Measuring jugs — for measuring liquids, e.g. milk.

Electrical Equipment Can Get Jobs Done *Faster*

Electrical equipment can help you chop, mix etc. more quickly and easily.

1) A food processor is just a jug with a rotating blade used to chop, blend or mix food. They can chop food quicker and more finely than chopping by hand.
2) Blenders are very similar to food processors, but they're designed to blend foods to a smooth texture, such as soups or smoothies.
3) An electric whisk makes whisking quicker and easier than whisking by hand.

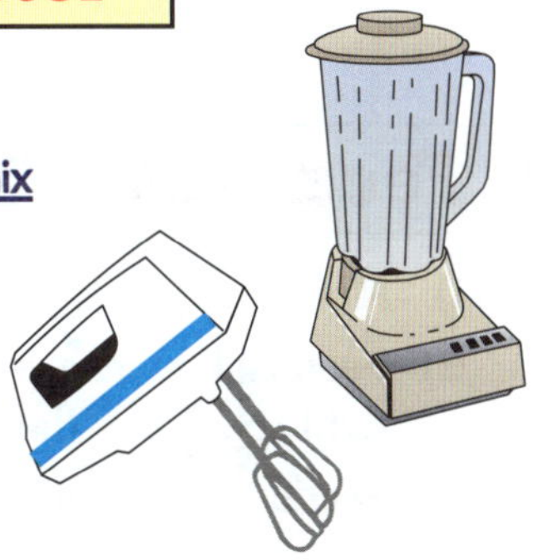

Use the *Right Equipment* to Make *Healthier Products*

Steamers are a good way to cook food such as vegetables, instead of boiling them in water.

1) Vegetables cooked by steaming (p.59) keep more of their taste, texture and colour.
2) They also keep more vitamins and minerals (lots are lost by boiling).
3) The food doesn't have to be drained so it's less likely to break up.

1) When you fry food in a normal pan, the fat you add helps stop the food getting stuck to the pan's surface.
2) Non-stick pans have a special coating to stop food sticking to the pan. So, using a non-stick pan means you don't have to use as much fat when frying — so it's healthier.

Get ready to cook up a storm...

That's the last page of the section folks... hopefully you've now got all the information you need to help whip up tasty, healthy meals for you and anyone else that comes knocking at the door. Remember to have fun, cook some tasty treats and don't be afraid to try out your own recipe ideas — you could be the next Jamie.

Section 6 — Cooking and Nutrition

Section 7 — Control and Design & Technology

Systems and Control

A lot of projects you do in D&T will involve electronic systems with inputs and outputs. It's important you know all about the different kinds, and how they're used in a number of different systems.

Systems are Made up of an Input, Process and Output

A system has various parts that work together to perform a set function. Systems can be broken down into these simple stages:

INPUT ➡ PROCESS ➡ OUTPUT

This is called a block diagram. Each block shows a "subsystem" — one part of the whole system.

1) The input is a signal, change in the environment, component or process that starts the system off. E.g. the dough fed into a bread machine or a button on a phone being pressed.
2) The process is what happens to the input to change it into an output. Information from the input controls the output. E.g. the skills and labour of the workers in a factory or the working of a computer processor.
3) The output is the result of the system. E.g. the final product on a production line or the sound of a fire alarm.
4) Electronic systems often contain a user interface. This includes a number of inputs and outputs that the user can interact with, e.g. the touchscreen of a smartphone.
5) In electronic systems, inputs and outputs can be a number of things, including movement (e.g. a fan), heat (e.g. a thermostat), sound (e.g. an electric keyboard) or light (e.g. safety lights).

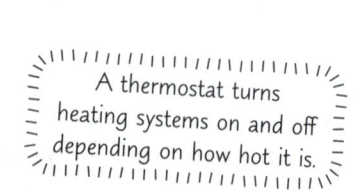

A thermostat turns heating systems on and off depending on how hot it is.

Feedback Makes Sure the System is Working Properly

1) More complex systems include feedback.
2) Feedback means checking the quality of the output, and, if it isn't right, changing the input. This is sometimes called feedback control.
3) Feedback can be done either by a person or electronically.

Some Common Electrical Inputs and Outputs

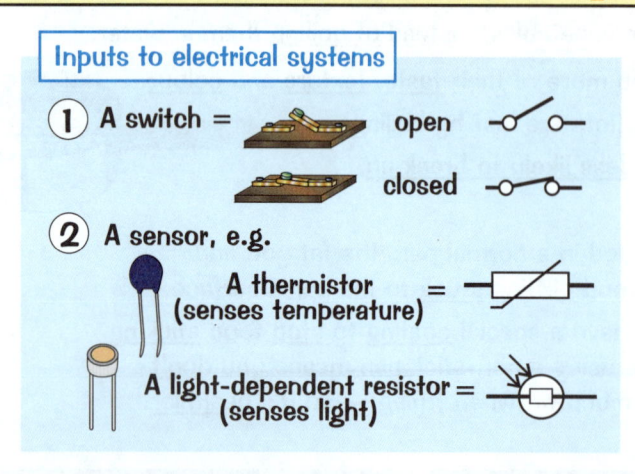

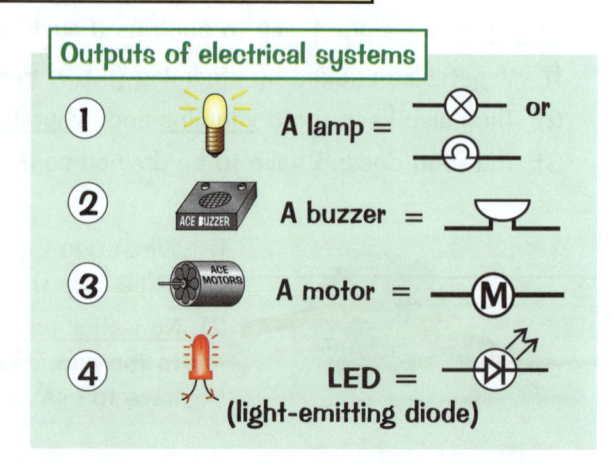

Inputs to electrical systems
1) A switch = open / closed
2) A sensor, e.g.
   - A thermistor (senses temperature) =
   - A light-dependent resistor (senses light) =

Outputs of electrical systems
1) A lamp = ⊗ or ○
2) A buzzer =
3) A motor = M
4) LED = (light-emitting diode)

When it all gets too much — you've got no sensor control...

A tricky topic this, so read it slowly and think it over slowly. It can be easy to get confused between what's an input and what's an output — see if you can scribble down a few of your own examples.

Circuits and PCBs

There are electric circuits in all sorts of products, e.g. toys, greetings cards and security systems. You can make your own electric circuits — including really posh ones with Printed Circuit Boards.

Electrical Circuits Can Be in *Parallel* or in *Series*

1) The electricity in a circuit comes from a battery or a power supply (e.g. mains electricity). The circuit can be wired so that electricity flows as a single stream of current (series circuit), or as a number of different branches of current — like different streams that form part of the same river (parallel circuit).

2) Christmas tree lights are an example of a simple electrical system that can be in parallel or in series. The switch is the input, the connection of the circuit is the process and the bulbs lighting is the output.

Series connection — if one bulb fails (breaking the circuit) all the bulbs go out.

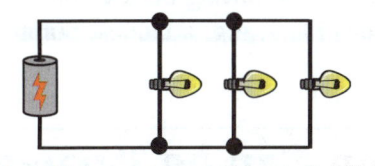

Parallel connection — if one bulb fails, the others continue to shine.

Mains electricity is the power supply you use when you plug something into a plug socket.

Switches are a Common Type of *Input Device*

1) Switches join two points of an electric circuit together. When the switch is closed electric current can flow around the circuit.

2) They can be used to control output devices in an electric circuit, e.g. a buzzer or motor.

3) Switches can be triggered by a number of different inputs, e.g. an oven thermostat is triggered by the temperature — when it's hot enough, a switch is opened and the heating element turns off.

4) These are three of the most common types of switch:

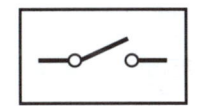

single-pole switch 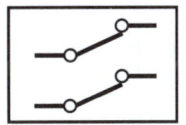   double-pole switch 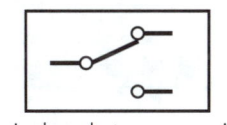   single-pole two-way switch

PCB Means *Printed Circuit Board*

1) Electric circuits are often made on a circuit board.

2) A prototype board or 'breadboard' is a basic circuit board that you can make your own circuits on. It's an insulating board with lots of little holes in it — you can push the legs of components through the holes and fix them in place. By connecting components on the prototype board with metal tracks, you can create a circuit.

3) Once you've tested a circuit on a prototype board, you could make a more permanent version called a Printed Circuit Board (PCB).

4) The circuit layout is transferred to a CAD package like ExpressPCB™. The circuit layout is printed onto a clear plastic sheet. This is the mask for the circuit board.

5) A piece of light-sensitive circuit board is exposed to ultraviolet (UV) light — with the mask between the board and the light. The pattern of the circuit is imprinted onto the circuit board.

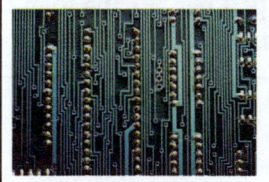

6) The board is developed and etched. The result is a pattern of copper tracks on the board — the basis of a circuit.

7) Holes are drilled in the PCB for the components, and they are soldered in place. The components are usually on top of the board and the copper tracks underneath.

Examples of Printed Circuit Boards (PCBs)

Short circuits — for the less fit among us...

Make sure the copper tracks on your circuit board don't overlap — or your design will short-circuit.

Section 7 — Control and Design & Technology

Motion and Mechanisms

Not all systems are electrical. You can also make mechanical systems. They work the same way — input, process and output. They're used to change the type or size of a motion and force.

There are Four Types of Motion in Mechanical Systems

1) Linear Motion — moving in a straight line, e.g. a rocket.
2) Rotary Motion — moving in a circle, e.g. a drill.
3) Oscillating Motion — moving backwards and forwards in an arc, e.g. a swing.
4) Reciprocating Motion — moving backwards and forwards in a straight line, e.g. a bicycle pump.

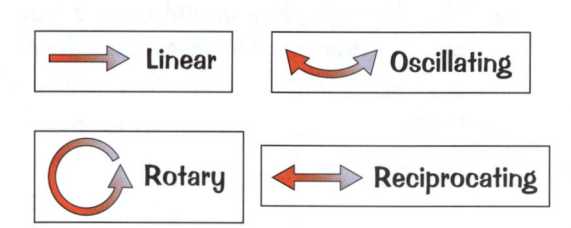

Input Motion Can be Turned into Output Motion

1) Mechanical systems change an input motion and force into an output motion and force.
2) They are designed to make things easier for you to do — they give you 'mechanical advantage'.
3) The process part of a mechanical system uses one or more mechanisms. Simple mechanisms you might use in your designs include:

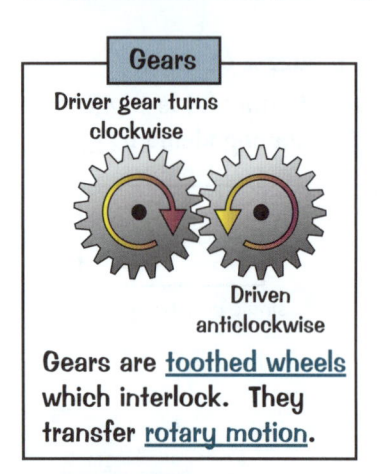

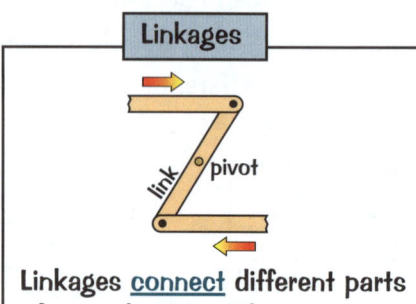

Gears
Driver gear turns clockwise
Driven anticlockwise
Gears are toothed wheels which interlock. They transfer rotary motion.

Linkages
Linkages connect different parts of a mechanism. They can transfer forces and change the direction of motion.

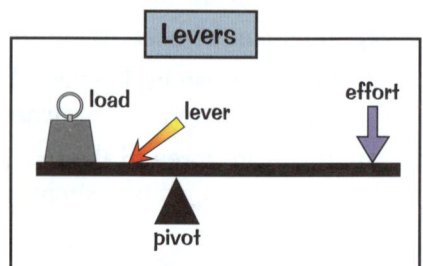

Levers
Levers enable an object to be lifted with less effort. As you move the pivot closer to the load it becomes easier to lift.

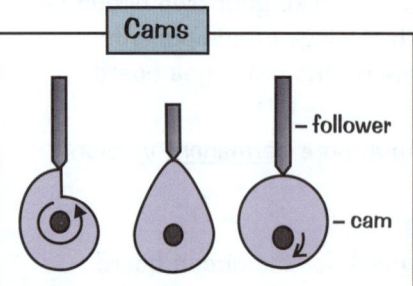

Cams
Cams change rotary motion into repeating motion. The cam mechanism is made up of a rotating shape and a "follower" which follows the shape of the cam.

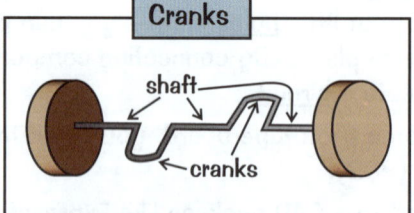

Cranks
Cranks can be as simple as a handle on a shaft. They turn rotary movement into reciprocating motion and vice versa.

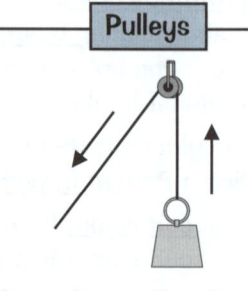

Pulleys
Pulleys change the direction of the force needed to lift the load — you can lift the load by pulling, rather than pushing.

Uplifting jumper — or woolly pulley...

Force is just the thump, push, pull, shove, whack, thwomp... the strength and power that are acting on an object. The force that little green man with a strange voice bangs on about is a whole different kettle of fish.

Section 7 — Control and Design & Technology

More Mechanical Systems

Mechanical systems are dead important and dead common — here's another page with some examples you might come across. Don't worry — you won't be asked to build a crane at the end of KS3 D&T.

Pulleys Can Reduce the Force You Need

1) A pulley changes the direction of the force needed to lift a load (see previous page).
2) Using two or more pulleys together makes things feel lighter than they actually are.
3) Using a double pulley (a fixed pulley and a moving pulley) means you only need half the force to lift a load.

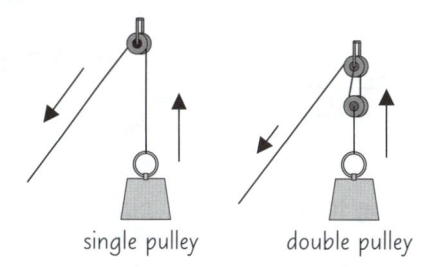

single pulley   double pulley

Bell Cranks are a Type of Linkage

1) Linkages (see previous page) change the direction of motion.
2) A bell crank changes the direction of motion through 90°.

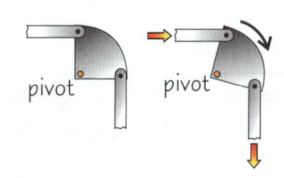

pivot   pivot

Pneumatic Cylinders Use Compressed Air

Compressed air is used to push a piston down a cylinder — air pressure is converted into movement.

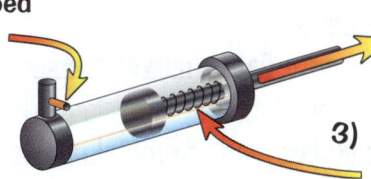

1) Compressed air is pumped into the cylinder here...
2) The pressure forces the piston out of the cylinder.
3) When the pressure's removed, a spring pushes the piston back into the cylinder.

Chain and Sprocket Mechanisms Transfer Movement

1) These are found on bikes.
2) Two sprockets (toothed wheels) are linked with a chain (made up from loads of links).

chain   sprocket

Mechanical Components Can be Combined in Systems

Cranes are systems that lift and move heavy loads.
1) They use pulleys to lift the load.
2) The top part of the crane rotates — this is done using gears.
3) The arm of the crane is a lever — the load is balanced with a concrete block.

I think I've cranked my sprocket...

Don't get your pulleys and your bell cranks confused, or all sorts of chaos might ensue. Time to reflect on a page full of the weird and wonderful mechanical systems you might come across during your KS3 D&T work.

Section 7 — Control and Design & Technology

Strong Structures

Structures are designed to carry loads and withstand forces without collapsing or falling over. Structures include anything from electricity pylons to buildings, cars, lamp-posts and thumbs.

Strong Structures Have to Resist Forces

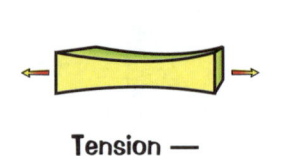

Tension — pulling force

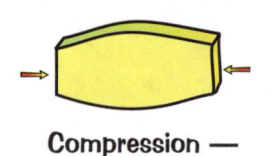

Compression — squashing force

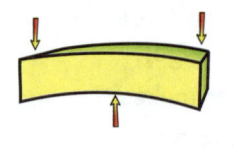

Bending force

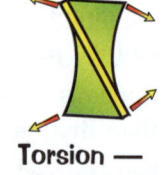

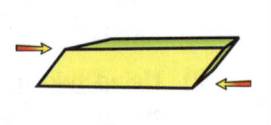

Torsion — twisting force

Shear — sliding force

Two Types of Structure — Sheet and Frame

Frame structures

1) A frame structure is a network of ties and struts joined together. Ties resist tension and struts resist compression.
2) Examples of frame structures include electricity pylons and houses built around a steel or wooden frame.
3) Often the frame is made up of triangular shapes, because they're strong. Using triangle shapes in a structure is called triangulation.

Sheet structures

1) Also called shell structures.
2) The structure is made up of flat or curved pieces joined together.
3) The way the pieces are put together is designed to make a strong, stable 3D shape.
4) Examples include car bodies made of metal panels, or moulded plastic traffic cones.

Test the Strength of Sheet and Frame Structures

1) You can compare the strengths of sheet and frame structures by doing a static load test.
2) Make a structure of each type out of card, wood or metal. To make it a fair test the structures should be the same weight and size, and made of the same material.
3) Balance a structure between two pieces of wood. The pieces of wood should be the same distance apart each time you do the experiment.
4) Place a small weight on top of the structure. Slowly add weights, until the structure collapses.
5) Record in a table how much weight it took to break the structure.
6) To make it a fair test use the same weights each time you repeat the experiment.
7) The more weight it takes to break a structure, the stronger the structure is.
8) Some materials, e.g. metals, don't break when a force is applied — they deform instead.

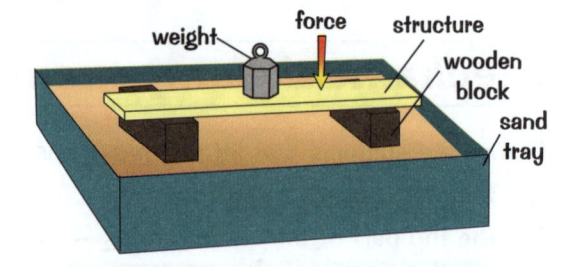

Weights can be a safety hazard. Carry out the experiment in a sand tray and on a firm surface. Wear safety goggles.

Twisted, retired skaters — Torsion and Dean...

Without force testing we'd have wobbly bridges, bendy lamp-posts and unsafe cars. That won't do, will it?

Section 7 — Control and Design & Technology

Computer-Controlled Systems

As we all know, computers will soon rule the world and stamp out humankind with a robot boot. But until then they can be very helpful little blighters when it comes to designing stuff...

Some Systems are Computer-Controlled

1) Computer-controlled systems use a computer to control the output device (no kidding).
2) Sensors are connected to the computer via an interface such as a control board.
3) These sensors detect inputs or changes in the outside world.

> **Example**
> Some traffic lights use a sensor to detect whether or not a car has pulled up. This controls whether or not they change colour.

4) The computer processes data from the sensors.
5) Computer-controlled systems often use embedded systems — these are small systems that do a specific task. Embedded systems often use small computers known as micro-controllers.
6) Micro-controllers can be programmed to perform a specific task, meaning that they can be used in a wide range of different situations and with a wide range of input and output devices. For example, they could be programmed to produce a sound or switch a light on.
7) Micro-controllers just have one specific purpose, meaning they're smaller, lower cost and lower power than general-purpose computers.

> **Example**
> Televisions contain a micro-controller that detects signals from the remote and works out what you want the TV to do (e.g. increase volume).

8) Once the information is processed, an output signal is sent from the computer to the output device.
9) Output devices that carry out specific actions are called actuators. They turn a signal into motion.

> **Example**
> A heat sensor detects that the temperature in a room is below a certain point. A micro-controller then turns on the actuator — the motor in an electric fan heater — and the fan starts spinning (and the heating element turns on).

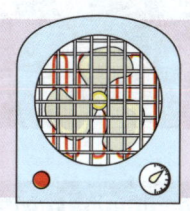

Robots are a Good Example

1) Robots are automated pieces of equipment which can carry out a range of tasks.
2) They are used to assemble products. They use a 'pick and place' system — picking up components in a set order and placing them together in a set pattern.
3) Feedback from sensors in the component trays or on the robot stops the assembly process if a component is missing.
4) The pressure of the robot's 'jaws', which it uses to pick up and move components, is controlled by pressure sensors. If the pressure is too high or too low, a signal is sent to a micro-controller, which in turn sends an output signal to the robot's jaws.

Pest control for farmers — the My Crow Controller 2000...

There you have it — computers control EVERYTHING. Well, maybe not everything, but MOST THINGS.

Section 7 — Control and Design & Technology

Security Control

A vast industry has built up around protecting our valuables. Of course in the good ole days you could leave doors wide open and possessions scattered over road. (Read in Yorkshire accent.)

Security Systems Protect People and Property

1) Security systems are used to protect people, equipment and property from criminals or misuse. They're used by both individuals and businesses.
2) There are a wide variety of security systems with several different control mechanisms (e.g. electrical, mechanical, computer-controlled and so on).
3) Common security systems include: smoke alarms, burglar alarms, coded (keypad) door locks, key-operated locks and combination locks on safes. Some dangerous machines have safety lock-out systems to prevent accidents.

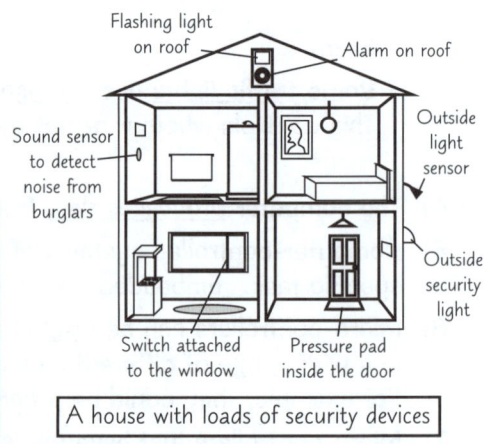

There are some legal constraints on security systems.
They shouldn't:
- harm people
- prevent authorised public access
- infringe on people's civil rights and liberties, e.g. hidden video cameras.

A house with loads of security devices

4) Security systems can be linked to form a more complex system. E.g. some security systems have a direct link with the local police station — the police are informed straight away if there's a break in.

Electrical, Mechanical and Pneumatic Locking Elements

Electric Locks 
1) These are often used as safety locks on machinery.
2) The lock is deactivated when an electric circuit is completed (or broken, depending on the lock).
   Example: A large press for making vehicle body panels can only operate if the electric switches in both the handles are gripped at the same time. This can only be done from outside the press, ensuring the operator's safety.

Pneumatic Locks 
1) Pneumatic devices use compressed air. The compressed air is stored in a tank and airflow is controlled by valves (one-way 'gates').
2) When the air is released it carries enough force to open or close a door.
3) The valves are often controlled with electromagnets.
   Example: Automatic train doors use pneumatic locking systems. They make it very difficult for someone to open a door while the train is moving.

Mechanical Locks 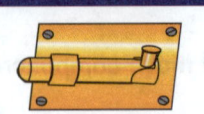
1) These are operated mechanically, either by hand or with a key.
2) They form a physical barrier.
   Example: Hand-operated bolts are placed at the top and bottom of a door to make it more secure.

It's simple — just live in a lead-lined bunker like me...

Security systems vary from simple mechanical systems to fully computerised electrical jobbies. Better security means cheaper insurance and less chance of a gap where your TV used to be — sounds ideal.

Section 7 — Control and Design & Technology

Monitoring and Display Systems

Aren't computers great? When they're not crashing, taking people's jobs or being programmed to kill the mother of the future human resistance leader, they can be used for some quite good stuff.

Control Systems Can Monitor the Surroundings

1) Monitoring systems can be automated — controlled by automatic equipment.
2) Monitoring systems have sensor inputs, a central processing circuit and an output. There is usually a feedback signal which can change the input.
3) Automated monitoring systems can be used to control an environment, e.g. whether a place is light/dark, warm/cold, dry/wet, noisy/quiet.
4) Monitoring systems can be used for care, e.g. monitoring the environment of a plant or pet to make sure the conditions are right.

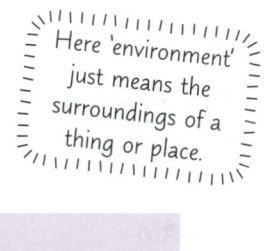

Here 'environment' just means the surroundings of a thing or place.

Examples:

The temperature of a tropical fish tank can be controlled by computer. A heat sensor senses if the water cools below a certain temperature, and a heater is turned on. When the water is hot enough, a signal from the heat sensor turns off the heater.

The light, temperature and amount of water given to plants in a greenhouse can be monitored and controlled with an automated system.

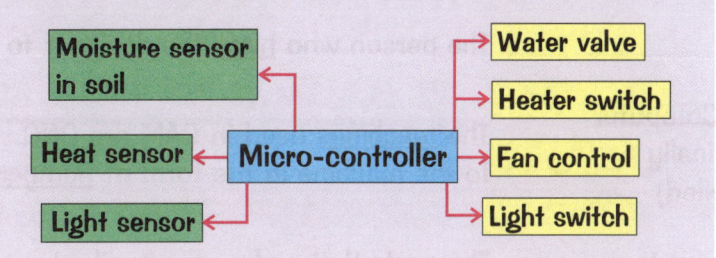

Inputs: Moisture sensor in soil, Heat sensor, Light sensor → Micro-controller → Outputs: Water valve, Heater switch, Fan control, Light switch

Control Systems Can be Used in Point-of-Sale Displays

1) Point-of-sale displays try to capture the customers' attention. They can be anywhere around a shop — in the window, in cabinets, on shelves or on counters.
2) They're designed for everyday use in the shop. They need to be fairly cheap because they get replaced regularly, and strong so they can stand up to everyday wear and tear.
3) Displays use many methods to try and grab attention, e.g.

- Bright colours
- Bold and eye-catching graphics (pictures)
- Highlighting product brands
- Electrical and mechanical control, e.g. controlled lighting, sound or movement.

4) An advantage of using control systems in a display is that they attract attention. Lighting and moving platforms can show off products to good effect.
5) A disadvantage of using control systems is that they are quite expensive to produce and have higher maintenance costs than a standard display.

I was ripped off by a short, beardy imp — a con-troll...

My tropical fish are thankful for the control system that keeps their water warm. I don't think their fishy brains quite grasp the full complexity of it though — they're still challenged by the pink castle.

Section 7 — Control and Design & Technology

Glossary

Actuator	An output device that carries out a specific action, in the form of a movement, when it receives an output signal.
Aesthetics	The look, taste, feel and smell of a product or material.
Batch Production	When manufacturers produce a group of identical products in one go.
Biomimicry	Copying nature to come up with designs.
CAD (Computer-Aided Design)	Using computers to design a product.
CAD/CAM	CAD and CAM joined together. This involves using specialised computer software to convert CAD drawings into instructions for machines.
CAM (Computer-Aided Manufacture)	Using a computer to control the machine making a product.
Client	The person who hires the designer to design a new product.
CNC (Computer Numerically Controlled)	The machines used in CAM are CNC. Data is sent to the machine in the form of numbers.
Components	The parts that make up a product.
Consumer	The user of a product.
Design Specification	A list of requirements for a product that is decided at the design stage.
Emulsions	Water and oil mixed together and kept together by an emulsifier.
Ergonomics	Making a product fit the user.
Feedback	Information, that comes from a system's output, that can be fed back into the process to change the input(s).
Fibre	A natural or man-made material that can be spun into yarn.
Function	The purpose and use of a product.
Iterative Design	A design process in which a single prototype is made, repeatedly tested and improved until all problems with it have been fixed.
Jigs	Guide tools — they make cutting and shaping materials quicker and more accurate.
Macronutrients	Nutrients the body needs in large amounts.
Manufacturer	A person or company that makes products to sell.
Mass Production	When manufacturers produce a product in large quantities. Also called high-volume production.

Glossary

Mechanism	A system made up of moving parts that performs a function.
Micro-controller	Small computer systems found inside many electrical or mechanical products, such as televisions and desk fans.
Micronutrients	Nutrients the body needs in very small amounts.
Mood Boards	A collection of photographs, colours and materials that shows the aesthetics wanted for a product.
Mould/Former	A hollow container used to form soft or molten material into a required shape.
Pneumatic	Something which works by using compressed air, e.g. a pneumatic lock.
Properties	The features of a material, e.g. strength, durability, absorbency and colour.
Prototype	A model of your design.
Quality Assurance	All the systems and procedures a manufacturer uses to make sure their products are high enough quality.
Quality Control	The physical checks a manufacturer makes to parts and products to make sure they are the right standard.
Resources	The materials, time, equipment and skills needed for making a product.
Risk Assessment	Identifying stages of the production process where there are hazards.
Seam	The join between two pieces of fabric.
Seasonal	Food that is only available at certain times of the year.
Seasoning	Ingredients added to food to flavour it.
Shelf-life	How long a product lasts before it deteriorates.
Smart Fabrics	Materials that change their properties in response to changes in their environment.
System	Various parts that work together to perform a function. They are made up of an input, process and output.
Target Group	The group of people you think will use a product.
Textile	A fibre, yarn or fabric.
Thermoplastics	Plastics that can be melted and formed into new shapes, e.g. acrylic, PVC, polystyrene.

Index

3D drawings 15
3D modelling 13
3D printers 26
6 Rs 29

A

abrasion resistance 43
accessibility 6
actuators 69
adapting designs 16
additives 55
advances in technology 4, 8
aesthetics 2, 3, 8, 10, 11, 31, 42
age groups 6
alarms 70
alloys 30
annealing 33
appliqué 46
Art Deco 17
Art Nouveau 17
assembly lines 25
automated systems 71
availability 11

B

baking 61
balaclavas 10
band saws 38
barbecuing 61
batch production 19
batik 46
Bauhaus 17
beetling fabric 45
bell cranks 67
bench grinders 39
bending 34, 68
biased information 5, 9
biodegradable 28, 29, 35
biomimicry 3
bits (drills) 38
blenders 63
block printing 46
blow moulding 33
boiling 59
Braille 6
braising 59
brushing fabric 45

C

CAD/CAM 14, 20, 26, 46
cams 66
carbohydrates 49-52
carbon fibre 32
casting 37
central processing circuits 71
chain and sprocket mechanisms 67
charts 15
chilling 21
chisels 39
circuit boards 65
circular saws 38
combining fabrics 45
communication 8, 9, 15, 16
competition 2, 8
composite materials 30, 32
compression 68
compromise 12
computer-aided design (CAD) 13, 24, 46
computer-aided manufacture (CAM) 18, 23, 24, 46
computer-controlled systems 69
computer numerically controlled (CNC) 26
consumer demand 8, 16
contacting experts 5
context design 1
continuous improvement 16
control systems 71
cooking methods 59–63
cotton 40, 41, 44, 45
cranks 66
crease resistance 43
creativity in design 2
cross-contamination 27
cultural values 6

D

dairy foods 50
darts 45
decorating techniques 46
deep-fat frying 60
deforming 37
design briefs 1
design movements 17
design specifications 10
dietary needs 6
disabilities (catering for) 6
display systems 71
downloading 5
drills 38
dry heat 61
durability 11

E

Eatwell Plate 50
electric locks 70
electrical circuits 65
electronic systems 64, 65
electroplating 35
emerging technology 4
environment 28, 29, 35
environment (impact of design and technology) 8
environmentally friendly 17, 28, 29
ergonomics 3
evaluating designs 16
evolution of products 16, 17
evolving technology 8
experts 5

F

fabric properties 40-45
fair tests 34, 43
farmers' markets 54
fats 49, 50
fatty foods 49, 50, 52
feedback 5, 14, 20, 64
feedback loops 19
ferrous metals 30
fibre (food) 49, 50
fibreglass 12, 32
fibres (fabric) 40
files 39
finishing 35
flow charts 12, 19
food colouring 55
food industry 24
food processing 21, 56, 57
forming 37
forums 5
frame structures 68
fruit 51
frying 60
functional foods 53

Index

G
Gantt charts 11
gathers 45
gears 66
generating ideas 2-4
glue 36
GM foods 28, 53
gougers 39
grilling 61

H
Halal 6
hand drills 38
hardening 33
hardwood 30
health and safety 12, 27
healthy eating 51
heat treatment 21, 45, 56
high-volume production 18

I
ICT 22, 24, 25
ideas boards 2
impact of design and technology 8, 9
industry jobs 22
ingredient properties 52
injection moulding 33, 37
inputs 64-66, 69, 71
inspiration for design 2, 3
inspiration from nature 3
Internet 5, 9
interviews 7
iterative design 14

J
jig saws 38
jigs 20
joints 36

K
knitted fabrics 40
knitting machines 26
knives 62
Kosher 6

L
ladles 62
laser cutters 26
lathes 26, 39
levers 66, 67
linkages 66, 67
locks 70
LYCRA® 44

M
macronutrients 49
man-made fibres 40, 44
manufacturing aids 20, 46
manufacturing specifications 11, 16
market pull 8
Marmite® 33
mass-produced goods 18
mass production 18, 23
material properties 11, 30-32, 40, 42-45
mathematical modelling 13
mechanical locks 70
mechanical systems 66, 67
memory cards 4
metal properties 33
micro-controllers 69
microfibres 44
micronutrients 49
microwaving 60
milling machines 26, 39
minerals 49
mixture fabrics 45
modelling 13, 14
modelling software 13
modern materials 32, 44
monitoring systems 71
mood boards 2
motion (in mechanical systems) 66, 67
moulds 20, 33, 37

N
nails 36
natural fibres 40
nutraceuticals 53
new ideas 2–4
new products 8
non-ferrous metals 30
novel foods 53
nutrients 49, 50
nylon 37, 40, 44

O
obesity 50
one-off production 18
outputs 64-66, 69, 71

P
packaging 28, 29
pans 63
parallel circuits 65
pasteurisation 21
patterns 3, 17, 46
pillar drills 38
pinking shears 48
plain weave 40
planes 39
planning 11, 12
    a meal 58
plastics 30, 31, 35, 37
pleats 45
plotter/cutters 26
plywood 30, 33
pneumatic cylinders 67
pneumatic locks 70
poaching 59
point-of-sale displays 71
pollution 28, 35
polystyrene 30, 37
polythene 30, 37
postmodernism 17
power drills 38
presenting ideas 15
preservatives 55
press moulding 37
pressing 48
printed circuit boards (PCB) 65
process (in electrical systems) 64
processed foods 52, 56, 57
product analysis 4
product testing 21
production lines 18
professionals 4
properties
    changing properties 33
    ingredients 52
    materials 11, 30-32, 40, 42-45
    metals 33
    resistant materials 30-32
    testing properties 34, 43
    textiles 40, 42-45

Index

protein 50, 52
prototypes 13
prototype boards 65
pulleys 66, 67

Q

quality assurance (QA) 20
quality control (QC) 20
questionnaires 7

R

recipes 58
recycling 29, 35
reforming 37
religious values 6
remote working 9, 22
repetitive strain injury (RSI) 9
repetitive tasks 23
research 1–7
    on the Internet 5
research and development 32
resistant material properties
risk assessment 27
rivets 36
roasting 61
robots 69
routers 26

S

saw benches 38
saws 38
scissors 48
screws 36
seam allowance 46, 47
seams 47
seasonal foods 54
seasoning 55
security systems 70
selecting materials 31, 42
sensors 69-71
series circuits 65
sewing 46-48
shallow frying 60
shape memory alloy 32
shaping materials 39, 45
shear (force) 68
sheet structures 68
simmering 59
sketches 13

smart materials 32, 44
social media 5
society (impact of design
    and technology) 8, 9
softwood 30
soldering 36
spatulas 62
specialist diets 51
spoons 62
spreadsheets 15
static load tests 68
steamers 63
steaming 59, 63
stencilling 46
stewing 59
stir-frying 60
structures 68
switches 65
systems 64

T

target groups 7
taste 55, 56
technology
    impact on design 4, 8, 9
    impact on society 9
tempering 33
templates 20, 46
Tencel® 44
tension 68
testing materials 34, 43
textile properties 40, 42-45
thermoforming 33
thermoplastics 30, 33, 37
thermosetting plastics 30
tie-dying 46
tolerances 11
tools 38, 39, 48
torsion 68
tucks 45
twill weave 40
type 2 diabetes 50

U

understanding needs 6
union fabric 45
uploading 5
user-centered design 3, 6

V

vacuum forming 19, 33
vegetables 40, 49, 50
Velcro® 3
video-conferencing 9
virtual models 13
vitamins 49

W

water resistance 43
welding 36
whisks 57, 62, 63
wood 30, 35, 36
workability 11
working drawings 15
world materials 41
woven fabrics 40